Dog Days in Andalucía

Dog Days in Andalucía

Tails from Spain

JACKIE TODD

MAINSTREAM
PUBLISHING

EDINBURGH AND LONDON

First published in Great Britain in 2010 by
MAINSTREAM PUBLISHING COMPANY
(EDINBURGH) LTD
7 Albany Street
Edinburgh EH1 3UG

ISBN 9781845966133

A catalogue record for this book is available
from the British Library

Typeset in Caslon and Garamold

Printed in Great Britain by
CPI Cox and Wyman, Reading, Berkshire RG1 8EX

3 5 7 9 10 8 6 4 2

For Stephen

Contents

Prologue

Islington, London, Early 1990s

'We can't have a dog in London: we're out all day, it just wouldn't be fair.'

'I know that.'

'When we live in Spain, OK?'

'Stephen. That will be written on my grave.'

'Please, don't start.'

'I'm not starting. Actually, I don't "start", as you put it. What sort of dog shall we get?'

'A Spanish pointer, of course.'

'What colour?'

'How do I know? It's not even born yet; in fact, its great-great-grandmother probably isn't either.'

'Can't you just dream? And, when we live in Spain, we can have a cat, too, can't we?'

'Of course.'

'Two. Two of those beautiful Mediterranean tabbies, the ones with the lovely charcoal stripes that match across their front legs, and the Cleopatra eyeliner.'

'Yes. When we live in Spain, OK?'

'Won't the dog have a problem with the cats?'

'Jackie, we have this conversation at least once a month. You know all of the answers to all of these questions.'

'OK. So it's all decided then: a Spanish pointer and two of those pretty little Mediterranean tabbies. Yes?'

'Yes. When we live in Spain. OK?'

'OK.'

I

Casa Rosa

We bought Casa Rosa as a home for holidays in the late spring of 1991. Stephen, quite rightly, calls that trip the most expensive holiday he has ever had. Earlier that year, against stiff competition, we had won the contract to design the new offices for the *Economist* magazine. I clearly remember sitting in the back of a black cab driving away from Duke Street, pissed off that I didn't have time to enjoy Selfridges, delighted to know that the job was ours, but less than impressed that it was going to be a very fast-track project. It would certainly mean that we would not be having a holiday that summer.

Stephen, with two colleagues, had started an architecture and office-design practice more than ten years earlier, and in the rather flashy and greedy '80s the business had grown as fast as the shoulder pads of the time. We worked together, which worked for us, but it did mean that mentally we were never out of the office. Twelve-hour days were normal, often followed by dinner with clients; weekends didn't exist. Our idea of a perfect evening was to curl up on the sofa, beans on toast balanced on our laps, watching anything on TV that did not require or provoke thought. Friends who lived far outside London went to more shows, concerts and exhibitions in a year than we had in our eight years in the capital. Our lives were the business – so our holidays were both precious and vital.

A couple of weeks later, *The Economist* lost the building they wanted and, knowing that there was going to be a pause, we grabbed at the chance of a quick break. Thelma, Stephen's mum, had for many years owned a charming little house in El Capistrano, one of the first developments in the hills just above Nerja, on the eastern Costa del Sol. We were on the first plane to Málaga the following day.

'We love Spain; we really should think about getting a place out here for ourselves.'

Stephen has a habit of coming out with these casual one-liners that sometimes change our lives. This, although I did not spot it at the time, was one of them.

It did make sense. We had cancelled numerous holidays, often at short notice and at great expense, to bow to the demands of our clients. A place of our own would give us so much more freedom. Our sightseeing days were over; we had both travelled extensively, been to almost every place on our 'must-see' list, and now, in no particular order, sun, silence and sleep were at the top of our holiday dreams. During that week, we looked at many houses and we found our first Antonio: Antonio the estate agent, a totally different animal to the English breed. Like all in his trade, he obviously wanted to sell us a house, but he genuinely came across as caring that we were going to be happy with our purchase and worked hard to that end. He enquired about our dream, our lifestyle, he collected us in his car, he bought us lunch and took us to every conceivable type of house. We saw beautiful places in the middle of nowhere, or so it seemed to me, at least 30 minutes along crumbling dirt tracks totally impassable in the winter rains, and an hour's drive to buy bread or milk. We looked at, and were sorely tempted by, a charming house that was accessed via the river-bed of the Rio Seco (*seco* means 'dry') and had been lovingly restored by its owner, Jesús. He had used traditional building methods as well as antique wall tiles, terracotta floors and old olive-wood beams to bring the house back to its prime, in the days when his grandparents had lived there. The only thing that really put us off at the time was the uncertainty of where the proposed future motorway would pass. Thank goodness it did, because after some much needed rain the following winter the river-bed of Rio Seco looked more like the Manchester Ship Canal, and now that the motorway is built it runs past the bottom of Jesús' orchard.

We viewed lofty penthouse apartments on the coast with jacuzzis on their enormous terraces and gold taps in every bathroom. Tourist ghettos: terraced houses that looked like whitewashed Coronation Streets blessed with sunshine and perma-tanned peroxide Bet Lynches behind every Black Horse, 'your-home-away-from-home'-type bar – no, thank you. We toured estates of newly built villas, complete with marble floors and aluminium double glazing, surrounded by ornate white railings topped by bronzed eagles. They resembled wedding cakes, and their private pools were overlooked on every side. No. Antonio even took us to Torrox Costa, a mere 15-minute drive from Nerja and home to half of Germany. There they don't give their high-rise flats names; with typical Germanic efficiency, they simply use numbers. Just imagine inviting friends to visit: 'You must come and see our new place, number 184 in block 17.'

That week we bought Casa Rosa. We had actually driven past it on our first day out with Antonio. I had noticed the For Sale sign and said that it looked interesting; this he had ignored totally. With hindsight, I think that he toured us around the area for a few days waiting to do a deal with the agent who had it on his books, because eventually he casually mentioned the place we had passed on day one and that, as I had expressed interest, he had arranged for us to see it.

It was beautiful: part of an old mill complex dating back to Moorish times. Nine steps led up to the heavy stable door, a door that we were soon to learn has a life of its own: it swells with the winter rains and withers in the blast of the summer sun.

This 'door with attitude' led straight into the kitchen, a rustic room with sloping beamed ceilings and a thick slab of olive wood, worn smooth over the years, that served as the breakfast bar. The owners proudly showed off the gleaming stainless-steel kitchen sink, pointing out that, at great expense, they had only recently replaced the old stone sink and its original brass taps. Even this couldn't put me off. The knobbly walls were at least two feet thick, their angles and bumps softened by probably thousands of coats of *cal*, the local lime wash. The wooden floors, very unusual for this area, still showed the well-worn paths of the mill workers, despite many layers of linseed oil and varnish. No two rooms were on the same level. There were two steps up to the bedroom off the kitchen – yes, a cosy but strange layout, I agree – then one step down to the little bathroom on the ground floor. If there were ever a 'Loo with a View' competition then I would enter the upstairs bathroom of Casa Rosa. From this elevated throne, the mountains soar and the sea twinkles in the distance. Outside there is a secret walled garden enclosing a wisteria- and vine-covered terrace threaded with winter jasmine and a jacaranda tree: this, for me, was the icing on the cake. It had only two bedrooms, ideally we were looking for three; there was no pool, we would have liked one. In fact, Casa Rosa was so far from the brief that we had originally given Antonio that both he and Stephen stared open-mouthed, then put their heads in their hands when I declared that this was it. It was perfect, ideal, just what we were looking for. My explanation that 'it just felt right' went completely over their heads.

Casa Rosa, in the tiny hamlet of La Molineta, situated just below one of Andalucía's famous *pueblos blancos*, the stunning white mountain village of Frigiliana. Only twenty minutes' drive from the coast, but a hundred years distant in lifestyle. This was my idea of Spain.

The water that used to power the mills still ran through the gardens, trickling over smooth worn stone, cooling and soothing the senses. Called the *acequia*, these waterways were built by the Moors in the tenth and eleventh centuries to bring the mountain water, via a network of tiny canals, to irrigate these valleys: an impressive feat of engineering even by today's standards. They were operated and controlled by a series of sluice gates, normally about three-feet-square sheets of rough metal that were padlocked in place to direct the water flow. The '*acequia* man' held the keys to these locks and would spend all of his days – and often parts of his nights, as well – going up and down the valley opening and closing the gates, altering the flow depending upon who was entitled to how much water and when. The value of a *campo* property – *campo* means 'countryside', but it is private land owned by families, passed down and divided, usually by word of mouth, through generations – around here has a direct correlation to the amount of water that it has been allocated and at what time. In summer, even if your water allocation is generous, if it is at midday it will evaporate rapidly and barely touch the dusty soil. One hour of water in the early morning or late evening is worth more than three hours mid-afternoon. These small irrigated orchards are mainly used for growing avocados, mangos, custard apples and *nísperos*. The best English–Spanish dictionary we have tells me that *nísperos* are the fruit of the medlar tree (which means nothing to me); they look and taste like small sweet apricots, are harvested in May and are said to aid digestion. Until moving here I had never seen a custard apple, here called a *chirimoya*: it is a large, rather ugly, gnarled-looking fruit that grows on tall, strong trees. If you think you might like puréed apple mixed with cold custard, then this is for you. Cut the top off as you would a soft-boiled egg, and eat it with a spoon.

One of these water-control points was almost directly under our bedroom window, and we soon grew accustomed to our 6 a.m. alarm call, which echoed down the valley: '*¿Tienes agua?*' ('Do you have water?') It was a regular part of life, and funnily enough, it became one of the many joys of our holidays: to be woken in such a different way from the usual screeching alarm clock, to note the fact that it was 6 a.m. and that the sun was rising. That we didn't have to hit Upper Street or the aggression of the Formula One track, once known as the M4, and then being able to turn over and sleep again, for as long as we wanted, was pure luxury.

Casa Rosa became our perfect bolt-hole from a hectic London life. We used it at every opportunity. In the year before moving here we made ten visits, sometimes for little more than forty-eight hours at a time. Every time we locked that old stable door and prepared to head back to the airport, I always found an excuse, any excuse, to rush back inside for something. We were then, and still are, Hispanophiles. Like every country, Spain has its faults, of course, but here we usually have to search to find them, then we quickly excuse and forgive them.

My first real experience of Spain, or rather my first real experience of real Spain, had been several years before we bought Casa Rosa, when Stephen brought me here as a surprise birthday treat in early March. The weather was a bonus; having left London in a blizzard, the sun was strong, and I got a genuine red nose on Red Nose Day. But it was when I discovered the trio of romantic Moorish cities, Córdoba, Granada and Sevilla, with their stunning architecture and proud sense of history, the openness and warmth of their people, and the delicious food that I began to realise that I had seriously misjudged this country. Had I paid more attention to my English Literature lessons, I would also have known much more. Writers flocked to Spain: Ernest Hemingway, George Orwell, Laurie Lee and many more had all fallen under the country's spell. Please indulge me here: thank you Mrs Hargreaves; you are most probably not around any more, but at Dorchester Grammar School for Girls in the late '60s, you somehow managed to teach a spoiled, arrogant little brat to love books. I will always be grateful.

Much, much earlier, my life as a stewardess had meant regularly spending an hour or ten on the tarmac at Málaga Airport, white gloves, American Tan tights and a fixed smile in place. The gloves and tights should give you a clue; it was quite a while ago. With this very limited exposure, I had decided Spain was somewhere that held no interest. Passengers on the outbound journey, having been up since at least three in the morning, were, in general, subdued; however, after two weeks of cheap everything, the return flights were often a nightmare. Even the teetotallers appeared out of it; their home-bound flight seemed to mark the grand finale of their well-earned holiday. Valiantly trying to cram stuffed donkeys, sombreros and castanets into the overhead lockers, clutching bottles of wine depicting their favourite English football teams and singing 'The Birdie Song', they were ready for their last party. Spain, and especially its visitors, I had long ago decided were not for me. How wrong could I be?

2

Southern Andalucía, 1997

In March of 1997, we realised our dream and finally moved to Spain. It is impossible to pinpoint the start of that dream. Yes, we loved the country in general and the area in particular, but more than that we had begun to become part of a small, close community. In London, we didn't know our neighbours; we were on polite nodding terms with the people next door on the rare occasions that our paths crossed. In contrast, within half an hour of opening the top half of Casa Rosa's door, we would find a bag of oranges hung on its handle. A trip to the village the following morning would bring warm greetings, smiles and 'we heard you were back' comments. The village telegraph amazes me to this day. Over time, we had learned these people's values and found that we shared them; I suppose they would be called the old-fashioned values now. We were surrounded by honest, hard-working people who treated each other with respect and care and richly peppered their lives with fun and celebration. Home became La Molineta, not our house in Islington. Casa Rosa had served us very well for six years, though once deciding to live here permanently, our needs were going to be different. Certainly we would need more space and a pool, but that house had a huge piece of our hearts. We were both so loath to leave all that behind.

With incredible luck, or good fortune, or you could even call it a twist of fate, at exactly the time we had been making the decision to leave the UK and start a new life here – not something we took lightly – the old bakery, La Panificadora, adjoining Casa Rosa was offered to us in a private sale. It was the first time it had been on the market since the owners had bought the whole hillside of crumbling mills more than 35 years before. Ever since buying Casa Rosa we had been asking Peter and Felicity, the owners of the rest of the hillside, if we could buy just three metres of the adjoining garden to give us enough space for a pool. The answer had always been a polite but very firm *no*. They had stumbled upon the mill buildings in the early '60s after a tip-off from Felicity's mother, Rose. The love of La Molineta that had grown over the 30 years they had spent restoring the buildings shone through not only in their stories but in the houses themselves, too. We felt honoured to be given the chance to own another of the houses. They knew we would treasure it, as, indeed, we do.

So the opportunity to buy La Panificadora was the tipping of the scales in our decision to move to Spain. It already had the essential pool, and we could then steal the much needed three metres from our own new home to put a pool into Casa Rosa. Holiday homes without pools understandably don't rent well. We could have our cake and eat it: let Casa Rosa earn its keep and therefore not have to sell it, and only have to move next door. We had loved The Pan, as it was known locally, since first entering it soon after buying Casa Rosa. Four bedrooms, two bathrooms, huge arched living spaces and a generous, terraced, walled garden. It was a most unusual building. Most old houses in the southern part of Andalucía look like a collection of shoeboxes. Rooms were added when needed and when money allowed; large spaces were not necessary: hard to heat in winter, redundant in summer. Our former mill was a rarity.

There was only one drawback: La Panificadora was rented to a holiday company until the end of that October, and we all agreed that the contract had to be honoured. It was ours on paper, we got the rental income, but we had a six-month wait to move in.

Knowing that we were finally on our way, busy selling and packing up in London, we had not been to Casa Rosa since the previous Christmas: only three months, but three months that had brought the wettest weather that part of Spain had seen for more than ten years, and delighted relief to the local farmers following a full five-year drought.

We had sailed from Portsmouth at 11 p.m. on Friday, 21 March, a date that since set four months previously had had stars and asterisks around it in my diary – the diary that also had a countdown list of the days and 'To Do' lists of epic proportions. Having grown up as a typical army brat, watching my mother pack us up and move every few months, the task of moving countries didn't daunt me; in fact, I really enjoyed it. We only had one problem: what to do with Nonnie. Nonnie, our British Blue cat, was almost ten years old at this point, and we had had her since she was a tiny kitten. Her pedigree name would not fit onto this page; she was stunningly beautiful and stunningly stupid in equal measure. With our London lifestyles we could only just juggle a cat into our busy schedules, but neither of us could imagine life in a totally animal-free zone. However, she was also not designed for the heat of Spain; her thick pewter-grey coat made me think she had been put through the upholstery department of the cat-making factory twice, by mistake. The problem was solved when my parents suggested that she follow their route and spend her retirement in Dorset, where she spent the last five years of her life indulged and contented.

So, although we had booked a cabin on the ferry, were tired and should have slept, we were both too excited. This was the first step of our long-planned adventure. We took our brandies to the stern, waved goodbye to our previous lives and toasted our future.

We arrived at Casa Rosa late on the morning of Sunday, 23 March after a 28-hour drive, almost without a stop, from the ferry port of Caen on the northern French coast. Not a journey to be recommended. At 2 a.m., just north of Madrid and exhausted after eighteen hours in the car, we agreed that doing the trip in one had been over-ambitious. Actually, this is not strictly true; I had said from the start that it was too long a drive and had suggested a stopover, which Stephen dismissed. So I was full of 'I told you so's when we decided to stop at the next hotel. There weren't any. Eventually we settled for an hour's doze in the car on the forecourt of a petrol station: easy for me; five foot four can curl up quite comfortably in a Land Rover, and my mother had always said I could sleep on a washing line. For Stephen's six foot plus, it was more difficult. Waking, we splashed water on our faces, scraped the fur off our teeth, drank nerve-rattling *café solos* and set off again. If you ever find yourself in the same situation, please do remember that, half an hour later, just south of Madrid, the road is lined with hotels.

Stiff, grubby, exhausted, but still elated, we gently coaxed Casa Rosa's old, wooden, rain-swollen stable door open enough for us to just squeeze through. Black velvet was very much in fashion at the time and, if nothing else, we were fashionable. Everything was covered in a good inch and a half of the stuff: a smelly, furry black mould. It blossomed from the walls, it powdered all the beds and linen right down to the underside of the mattresses, it had turned the beige sofas black and it had even grown on our toothbrushes. When we opened the wardrobes, every single item of clothing was black stinking velvet. Every light we turned on blew, showering us with glass and black mould. The first two weeks were a blur of bleach and black bin bags.

At the end of each long day – days that felt like hard labour in comparison to our office-bound previous lives – we repaired to Antonio's bar, less than a minute's walk away, for a medicinal brandy. Antonio would fish his penknife out of a pocket and cut us a few slices of crusty bread to accompany a goat's cheese stored in olive oil so strong that your mouth would feel as if it had just sucked a lemon and a peppery chorizo sausage. Watching the setting sun turn the mountains first pink, then purple, and with its promise to return tomorrow, we listened to the goat bells in the distance, watched the mules silhouetted on the horizon carrying their loads home and soon remembered why we had chosen to move to this perfect place.

3

Antonio and his Bar

Antonio and his bar: both have been, and, in fact, still are, pivotal to the informality of our life here. To Antonio, all the clichés apply: he's a loveable rogue, a rough diamond, a tinker with a heart of gold and an eye to a deal. Years ago, before we grew wise to such things, he warned us of the dangers the rotting old ox cart in front of our house could cause. We were actually rather fond of it. Eventually, for a fair price, he agreed to get rid of it – then sold it to our neighbours. Like most of his generation, he has the sort of olive skin that makes a weathered orange look smooth, and the bloodshot, bloodhound eyes that can only be achieved after many years of sun, sex and sangria. At about five foot four, he is of average height, carries a bit too much weight around his middle and nearly always wears a hat: straw for summer, a new one every year or two, then, as the seasons change, an old grey-felt fedora that has seen many winters. It is rumoured that he was the local Romeo, especially for the first foreign women who moved here in the '60s. To be fair to him, the twinkle of the jet-black eyes can still be there at times, and once he has decided that you are his friend, you can do no wrong.

His long-suffering wife, Rosario, was born in La Molineta in 1937, the only person to have lived all her life there, and she never lets anyone forget it. Every morning I would watch from our kitchen window as she brushed the dust from the road in front of the bar onto the edge of her neighbour's land. An hour or so later, every morning, the neighbour's wife, Pilar, would come out and brush it back again. They could each brush into the gutter, but no – and yet they are still firm friends, have been so from childhood, and never speak of such things.

When we arrived that March, Rosario was recovering from a very badly broken ankle. She had fallen while picking avocados in the valley and, knowing that Antonio would be in the bar all day, she had dragged herself up to the roadside. Even now she still has a pronounced limp and uses a walking stick. She was staying with her daughter, María, in El Morche, a small and rather ugly village on the coast road back towards Málaga. Like most Spanish villages, the industrial and commercial areas are on the main road, but whereas a little exploring will usually uncover pretty squares and churches, El Morche has none: what you see from the road is as good as it gets.

Hobbling on crutches, there was no way she could negotiate the steep rough track down to her house below the bar. María's flat, on the third floor, has only two bedrooms, and their son, evicted from his room, was sleeping on the sofa. María loves her mother dearly, but not when she is in her house 24 hours a day and has a moody displaced teenager to placate, and Rosario was missing La Molineta. We had begun to convert the ground floor of Casa Rosa into a flat, with the idea that my mum might move out here some day, or at least for the winters, something she was still blowing hot and cold about at the time. The bedroom and bathroom were finished, and our offer that Rosario might like to spend a few days in our basement was greeted with enthusiasm by all concerned, especially María (although I suspect that Antonio's smile was rather forced; he was rather enjoying his newly discovered freedom). Rosario moved in the next day and stayed for nine months.

Antonio's bar is about 12 feet square and opens straight onto the road. It has two tiny wooden tables and six mismatched chairs, a mirror that advertises a long-forgotten gin company, and many pictures of Franco torn from old newspapers and tacked to the nicotine-stained walls. He opens when he gets up and closes when the last person leaves, often at two or three in the morning. A few years ago, he acquired an old cassette player and delighted in becoming the 'disco' of La Molineta, playing crackling *sevillana* and *cante jondo*, the raw flamenco of Andalucía, at full volume. We have always suspected that he has never learned to read or write but, like many of his age around here, has become adept at disguising the fact pretty well. In 1997, all drinks were 100 pesetas: water, wine, beer or brandy. He keeps a piece of chalk behind the bar, and for every drink ordered, he makes a mark on the bar top in front of you. At the end of the evening, he counts the marks, multiplies by 100, and that is your bill.

One evening, about three weeks after our arrival in late March, we stood, still smelling of bleach, in the doorway of his bar, watching dark blue-black clouds building up ominously behind the mountains.

'Is it going to rain, Antonio?'

He grunted, scratched his stomach, his crotch and then his stubbly chin; he was obviously giving the question some quite serious consideration.

'Yes. But not until the end of October.'

That evening, Antonio decided that now we were *aquí para siempre* (here for ever), it was time to introduce us to the local wine of Frigiliana: in this case, his home brew. Wine – no problem – I often used to share a bottle or two with girlfriends after work and still be able to walk in a straight line. *Vino de terreno* (wine from the earth), however, proved to be an entirely different concoction, and I honestly don't remember leaving the bar or getting to bed that night.

4

Dog? What Dog?

The following morning at about half past ten, the sun was celebrating my discomfort, sneaking through chinks in the bedroom curtains and drilling into my poor bloodshot eyes. There comes an age when recovering from the excesses of the night before gets harder, and I had to face the fact that I had reached it. With totally unnecessary noise and flourish, Stephen banged a cup of black coffee on my bedside table.

'The dog's here and it's gorgeous. I think we should keep him.'

'Dog? What dog?'

'The one you said you would take to the animal-rescue charity.'

'When?'

'I don't know when.'

'No. *When*. When did I see a dog I said I would take to animal rescue?'

'Last night in Antonio's, to the holidaymakers who had seen it thrown out of a car, remember?'

'Umm.'

'They've been feeding it for almost a week, but they go home today. They said it would break their hearts and ruin their holiday if they just walked away not knowing what would become of it, remember?'

'Umm.'

Wrapped in a towel, I shuffled downstairs, still clutching my coffee. The dog stood in the kitchen looking at me. It gave a small, nervous wag of its tail, head on one side. Considering that I had gone to bed in full make-up and now resembled Coco the Clown, he was obviously a very polite little boy. My first dog. For both of us, it was love at first sight.

Bad hangovers definitely demand hearty food, and with only this thought, we popped the puppy on the back seat and drove up to El Cerro, one of our favourite restaurants at the time, with its views to the sea and the backdrop of mountains, mama in the kitchen and the sons and daughter serving. Esperanza's cooking would do the trick.

Volumes have been written about how to get your new dog used to car journeys. 'Let doggy sit in it for a few days before you ever even think of driving it anywhere.' Then, 'take the car around the block a few times, driving slowly, nothing more'. Sorry, puppy, we need food. These were the days before this quaint family restaurant displayed a list of do's and don't's as long as your arm, had a menu in English and 'No Dogs' signs on every surface. Also the days before Judith Chalmers featured it in some travel programme as one of the unspoiled jewels of the area, always the kiss of death. The puppy wandered around happily.

'What's his name?'

'Sorry?'

'The puppy. What's his name?'

The fuchsia-pink, freckled seven-year-old with ginger hair and two earrings, wearing an Arsenal shirt, did actually have a point.

'What shall we call him?'

'Patch.'

'No.'

'Dog.'

'Don't be stupid.'

'Remember Gordon at work? He had a dog called Baxter. It's a good name. Baxter.'

'He's not a Baxter.'

'Well, he can't be a Blackie or a Spot or a Snowy or something; he's every colour. How about Patchwork? You enjoy sewing.'

At this stage, as you can tell, our brains were not exactly firing on every cylinder. So, resorting to the hair of the dog with no name (excuse the pun), we ordered a bottle of *vino rosado* and, after much creative thinking, we decided to call him Charlie.

That should have been more than enough for one day. But Stephen, knowing about such things, decided that in the evening we should take Charlie to a vet to 'just have him checked out', whatever that meant. There are three veterinary practices in Nerja, our nearest town, and we chose at random. Luck was, as usual, with us. Rafael and Dolores are a husband-and-wife team whom, although we didn't realise it at the time, we now would not be able to do without. While Stephen toured the town looking for parking, I carried Charlie inside and was shown straight into the consulting room. I explained, in poor Spanish, that he was an abandoned puppy, that we intended to keep him and that we just wanted to make sure that he didn't have any major health problems. Rafael gave him a thorough examination: eyes, ears, hip joints, thermometer(!) and a blood test. To break the silence:

'At least he seems to have been well fed. He has a very fat little tummy.'

'*Parásitos.*'

'*¿Cómo?*'

'He is fat because of *parásitos. Parásitos.* I give injection.'

With that, he used a syringe-type pump to force some white gunge down Charlie's throat. It marked the beginning of his pathological hatred of the vet; nowadays, if I even drive down the same street, Charlie howls. Spanish dogs have passports – or at least they should – and Rafael proceeded to make one out for Charlie, estimating his age at about six weeks. He flicked back through his desk diary and, without a word, gave him a birth date of 22 March, the day we had landed in Spain. I just love fate and the tricks it can play. Back in reception, Stephen had arrived. We paid the bill (less than it would cost to treat a goldfish in the UK) and celebrated by buying a smart little red collar with matching lead and a wicker dog basket with, strangely, pictures of cows in a meadow on its cushion.

Having made a rare evening journey into town from our relatively rural retreat, we decided to stay for tapas and watch the world go by. We sat at one of the many pavement cafes. *Tapa* is Spanish for 'lid', and the tradition of eating a tapa with your drink dates back to the times of travel by coach and horses. Drinks would be brought to the travellers and, to keep the dust out, a little saucer was put over the glass. Over time, as competition grew between these inns, a slice of tortilla or ham was added for free. If you know where to go around here, you can still get a free tapa with every drink. In the tourist bars, they charge outrageously. Our Spanish friends wouldn't dream of drinking anything alcoholic without a tapa to accompany it; don't drink on an empty stomach is something that we British preach and they practise.

I showed Stephen Charlie's passport. 'Look. Charlie is all official now; he has a passport.'

'Charly?'

'Yes, we agreed at lunchtime: Charlie.'

'Charl*y*. Charlie with a *y*.'

'Let me see. Oh. Oh well, OK, I didn't notice. Anyway, I'm sure he won't mind; it sounds the same. The vet was very kind, gentle and thorough, and he said Charly has something called *papasitos*, but that we weren't to worry. He gave him some stuff and said he will be fine.'

'You mean *parásitos*: that's worms.'

Right on cue, Charly realised that something volcanic was

happening at his rear end. The action of him trying to turn around and investigate this new sensation resulted in an arc of . . . well, I am sure you can imagine. We threw a 1,000-peseta note on the table as both payment and apology, picked him up carefully and ran.

5

Life with a Dog

So we had Charly. Not the Spanish pointer we had so long imagined, not anything that you could really call a breed. Perhaps one day a Labrador may have met his great-great-grandfather, who may have had a passing fling with a German shepherd, but that's about as close as we can guess. With all the colours of a herd of goats and sad, almost transparent, pale hazel-green eyes, Charly was born frowning, looking old and worried. The only really remarkable thing about him at this stage was his incredibly pink nose. Our French neighbour has always called him Truffe Plastique because his nose really does look just like one of the pink plastic ones we used to stick onto potato men when we were kids. In the days before Game Boys and computers, potatoes could really be very entertaining.

The following day, Stephen left early. He had an ongoing project and the client refused to deal with anyone but him, so for our first six months here he commuted between Málaga and London, spending four working days and three nights, every other week, in London. He hated going, but in a classic case of leaving full-time employment one day and coming back as a consultant the next, it was just too lucrative to turn away.

That morning, the builders arrived. Just a 'normal day in the life of . . .', but both dogs and Spanish builders were new to me. The team of four started at eight, by which time most of

them had had at least two very strong *café solos* and one, maybe
two, brandies or *anises* to 'help their digestion'. The project was
a simple one, certainly compared to what we have done since. We
wanted to remove the window in the dining room and replace
it with glass-panelled doors that would lead straight onto the
terrace. Well, the coffee, the brandy or perhaps just the basic
Spanish machismo certainly worked. Within five minutes the
window and the wall below it were gone, replaced by a gaping
hole and a pile of rubble. Then it started to rain. Not rain as we
knew it from England – just a drizzle, really – but, with much
sucking of rotting teeth and shaking of heads, they packed up
and left. I chased after Bigote, another Antonio, less than five
feet tall and nicknamed for his impressive big black *bigote*, his
moustache.

'Antonio. What's happening?'

'It's raining.'

'I know, but why are you going?'

'It's raining.'

'I'm sorry, I don't understand; my Spanish isn't too good.'

'It's OK. I prefer my women not to speak.'

They left.

Then the rain really started to practise for England: it poured
down. There was a hole in the dining room that you could drive
a car through and, to add to the work for my mop and bucket,
nobody had bothered to mention toilet training for dogs.

Using the mobile with the dodgy connection – we didn't have
a landline at the time – I called Stephen.

'The builders have gone.'

'They'll be back tomorrow.'

'There is a huge hole in the wall.'

'Not for long.'

'It's raining.'

'It'll stop.'

'Charly keeps peeing inside.'

'Take him outside.'

'But it's raining.'

'Sorry, can't hear you, you're breaking up. Call later, love you, bye.'

Bastard. By now you can probably spot the optimist in this relationship.

We had given no thought to food for our newly acquired pet. I was 20 minutes' drive from town but without a car. For three days, Charly ate cornflakes soaked overnight in milk for breakfast, tuna for lunch and hot-dog sausages for supper. Hot dogs are still his all-time favourite food.

During those first six months, every other Thursday, late in the afternoon, I would get a phone call.

'A story of civil war, of a quixotic battle against nature and loss.'

'No, I don't think so.'

'Harry Silver has it all: a beautiful wife, a wonderful son, a great job in the media – but one night he throws it all away.'

'Perfect. Yes please.'

'The spare narrative hides a commitment to his subject that pulls you in and leaves you gasping.'

'Sounds a bit heavy.'

This was Stephen standing in the W.H. Smith at Heathrow's Terminal Two and trying to keep me supplied with books. I have always enjoyed reading, but now, with no television, no computer, a dodgy phone line seriously impeding my habitual two-hour phone calls to friends and six nights a month on my own, I was getting through more books than ever.

When Stephen was in London, Charly kept me sane and also made me eat my words. Never having had a dog in my life, I could put up a pretty good case for the superiority of cats. Cats are independent, self-sufficient and selective in the objects of their attentions and affections. This is all true, and I adore them, but Charly was such a good companion. He listened to my every word, treating even my most inane comments like pearls of wisdom. He followed me everywhere: even when I told him that I was only going into the kitchen and would be back in seconds, he insisted on coming with me. My choice of music suited him just fine; he never changed the disc for Janis Joplin or Crosby, Stills and Nash. Within days of his arrival, I couldn't remember or imagine life without him.

6

We Live Here

For the first couple of months, life was just an extended holiday. There was no plan for each day. Bumping into friends in town could often lead to a lunch on the beach, which would finish at about four or five, an invitation to come back for a sundowner, and the day was all but gone. Fine for holidays, but we soon realised that to live here permanently and, ideally, to share this new life with our livers, something would have to change.

Of course, it is perfectly possible to live on the Costa del Sol without really letting the fact that it happens to be in Spain intrude at all. We have met many people who do just that. Twelve years ago, the English newspapers didn't arrive until late the following day. There were very few supermarkets – you actually had to play charades in the shops to get served and, shock horror, very few Spanish spoke any English. There were, and still are, the delights of the brand names. The fact that the bestselling brand of coffee is called Bonka, the brandy to drink with it Soberano and that sliced bread is Bimbo is only surpassed by the perfect product with which to wash one's dirty knickers: the washing powder Colon. Now, of course, hypermarkets abound, and you can pick up your English pension at the local post office (not, I hasten to add, that I am anywhere near to doing that). There are also more courses teaching the Spanish to speak English than the other way round.

I recently phoned an English friend who was full of the cold to ask if she needed anything in town. Later:

'Hi, how are you feeling? Here's the butter you wanted.'

'Oh, *Spanish* butter.'

'Yes.'

'What's it like?'

'Butter.'

'Oh.'

She has lived in Spain for 18 years.

Like most places in the world where there are Brits, there is snobbery, too. If your car has English number plates, it usually means that you are here for more than the packaged two weeks (we may talk to you). If your licence plate is actually registered here and your car has hubcaps (hire cars don't seem to have hubcaps for some reason that I have never discovered), then you probably at least own a property and come out regularly (we may invite you for drinks). If you have a dog in the car, then the odds are that you live here; either that or are totally mad, besotted with your pet and and have gone through all the complications necessary to bring the mutt on holiday. However, we will risk it and probably, within a week, become lifelong friends. God help you if the vehicle has easyCar written down the side and, one summer, even worse: 'easyCar – please bring me back clean'.

In the first couple of months, with Charly installed in the car, we received more invitations from expats than we could believe. Drinks, dinner, supper, lunch, pool parties, bridge evenings, golf (I will return to that last one). We had thought that London had given us a good social life, but this was Hollywood comes to Spain. To be fair, we met some very charming and interesting people, but decided pretty early on that for us to get the most out of living in Spain meant living with the Spanish people and working hard to learn and embrace their culture and their language.

We were never couch potatoes in the UK, but we were office potatoes. We lived in Islington and worked in Smithfield, a stone's throw from the meat market and only a mile from home. I walked to the office once, on a Monday morning, full of good intentions. It was the same morning that I had half a grapefruit and a decaffeinated coffee for breakfast, and only one cigarette before I left the house. I think it may have been early in 1995. Normally, we drove to and from the office and caught taxis to and from meetings.

But now we lived in Spain and had a dog. More than a dog, really; Charly was a mind reader and our personal trainer. He seemed to know if we were thinking of not bothering with a walk that day: he would sigh loudly, flop down by the kitchen door with his head on his chubby baby paws and look up at us with those sad pale eyes. It worked every time. From Casa Rosa it is an easy but very steep walk down to the normally dry river-bed. A left turn and we walked upstream on a route that many hours later would have found us in Granada.

When we started this regime, Charly was about four months old, and we would walk for an hour at the gentle pace dictated by our puppy, then turn for home. Within three months, we were covering our hour's walk in twenty minutes. Younger and, we had always thought, fitter friends visiting from England were left panting at the wayside. I had joined London gyms and hated them, but walking amongst the pink and white oleander, crushing thyme, lavender and rosemary underfoot, didn't seem like exercise. Between us, we lost four stone in six months without any conscious effort and felt brilliant.

7

Learning the Language

In 1994, we had started taking Spanish lessons after work in the office. Julia, our teacher, is actually German. She grew up in Argentina – don't ask, I never have – and was funding her way through university by teaching languages. She was a good teacher. We were bad pupils. The theory was six until seven thirty twice a week, and then she set homework; it was like being back at school. It felt strange that I could leave a meeting where we had just been discussing a client's budget in hundreds of thousands of pounds and, within minutes, I would revert to being a 12-year-old, dredging up all the long-forgotten excuses for why I hadn't done my homework.

Lessons took place in the glass-fronted conference room, which meant that anyone passing could, and would, just pop in. Meetings ran late, and often we were just too tired to concentrate. Julia usually took all of this with good humour and did manage to instil the basic disciplines of Spanish grammar while we polished off a bottle of Pata Negra, a full-bodied red Valdepeñas that I can thoroughly recommend. Fuelled by the wine, we would have halting conversations on every subject: philosophy, the economy of Chile, women's rights. One evening, following the latest interruption, Julia banged the table in frustration.

'You two destroy all the order and discipline of my lessons. In Spain, you wouldn't even be able to buy a pair of shoes.'

A few weeks later, we returned from a trip to Salamanca, as always with a present for Julia. This time it was a pair of soft suede shoes, though she was right: we had struggled to buy them.

Three years after we moved here, she and her delightful Chilean husband, Moyses, came to stay with us for a week. On their second night, we invited four friends from the village to join us for supper. It was one of those occasions when everyone and everything gelled. We sat under the velvet sky with good food, great company, lots of wine and laughter. Then I spotted Julia at the other end of the table, giggling at overhearing my conversation with Javier.

'Julia, stop it, please don't laugh at my Spanish.'

'I'm not.'

'Yes, you were, I'm doing my best.'

'Your Spanish is brilliant, honestly it is, I'm really impressed, but your accent is appalling, you sound like a peasant.'

She went on to explain that we sounded like the equivalent of very fluent English-speaking Spaniards who had learned the language in Glasgow (for Glasgow read Frigiliana) and that she wouldn't be seen dead with us in Madrid. While Julia, to her credit, had hung in there and taught us the basics years before, most of our Spanish has been picked up here in Andalucía and is therefore of the dialect known as 'Andaluz'.

Unless you are one of those irritatingly fortunate people for whom foreign languages come almost naturally, which to me they certainly do not, then you will probably have your own cringe-making horror stories. My simple early mistakes, such as 'goodnight, I'll have a chicken exit' to a smiling waiter, pale into insignificance compared with one of my attempts at a conversation with Antonio – he of the bar – within a month or so of moving here.

He and Rosario live across the road and below the bar, at the end of a rough track. Their little house has an outside toilet and kitchen – yes, an outdoor kitchen. They have a mule, an old bow-backed horse, a pig, numerous cats and kittens, dogs and puppies, rabbits, birds and several chickens, all living so close to them that we call it Animal Farm.

It was raining on the morning that Antonio brought the eggs; the builders had just left. Again, it was only a drizzle, but enough to scare off the builders and bring the men out of the fields and into the bar. The top half of our stable door was open, and he leaned in with the carton of eggs.

'Hello, Antonio, come in out of the rain.'

'Where is your husband?'

'In England.'

'Then I will not enter, thank you. Take these. They are this morning's lay, still warm.'

'Thank you.'

He hurriedly pushed the carton into my hands and almost ran down the steps, calling out behind him that he would like the egg box back when I had the time. Later it was explained to me that a man seen calling on a woman with a gift when her husband was away was a cause for scandal.

I transferred the eggs into a bowl; they were still warm and stuck with little downy feathers. An hour later, having perfected my *thank yous* with the help of the well-worn dictionary and *501 Spanish Verbs*, I returned the egg carton to the bar, which was heaving. Any 12 people would make a bar of that size heave, and 12 Spaniards made it sound like a riot. Silence fell. Not just a woman entering the bar alone, but a foreign woman. I summoned up my perfectly rehearsed sentence as I put the carton on the bar.

'Antonio, thank you very much for giving me your beautiful big brown eggs; they look delicious.'

There was silence – at least a minute of it – as I walked away. Antonio had smiled, his eyes had twinkled, but he had not said a word; then, from behind me, the bar shook. The laughter startled the mules tethered to the railings and made the mule-dogs bark with excitement. Walking back up the steps to our house I met Mayte, our good neighbour, who during her time in Paris had somehow learned a lot of English, which she liked to practise with me.

'It's raining a little. The men have fun in the bar.'

'Yes. Antonio brought me some eggs earlier. I have just returned the box; they seem to think it's funny.'

'Why? What did you say?'

'I thanked Antonio for giving me his beautiful big brown eggs and said they looked delicious.'

'Ahh.'

'"*Muchas gracias para dar me tus huevos grandes y marrones, parecen deliciosos.*" That's right, isn't it? I looked it all up.'

She smiled. 'Yes, that is right enough; but tell me, in England, is there a slang or rude word for testicles?'

'Balls.'

'In Spain, it is eggs.'

We are Dying to See You

My definition of a true friend is someone you could call at four in the morning, say '*help*' and they would be there as soon as humanly possible, no questions asked. Someone whom you may not even see for a year or two and yet within minutes of meeting up again, it is as if you have never been apart. I consider Stephen and I lucky in that we have three friends of that calibre in the UK and have made two more since moving to Spain. Outside of them, we knew lots and lots of people, people we liked very much, people we would see pretty regularly in London. Naturally enough, in the growing euphoria of our imminent departure, we both threw out casual invitations to come and visit at every opportunity. And they came. Some even made it here before our furniture.

When the phone rang two days before the Easter holidays, Stephen was yet again at the airport picking up our latest visitors. In fact, he spent so much time there in the first two years that the airport police pulled him over to enquire about his running of an illegal taxi service.

'Hello, thought we'd let you know we are just approaching Fungi Rola.'

'Umm, who *is* this?'

'Oh, sorry, it's Easy Move here, like, Dennis, with your furniture, like.'

'Great, so you'll be here within a couple of hours.'

'A couple of minutes more like.'

'We are in Frigiliana.'

'Yeah, like I just said, we're really close, so, like, how do we, like, find you, like?'

'You are the wrong side of Málaga.'

'No, we are very close to Funga Lola.'

'We are in Frigiliana, at least an hour and a bit *east* of Málaga.'

'Shit, like. Sorry, like.'

When they did arrive, they were darlings, took one look at the steep stairs to the house, announced them to be no problem, then looked very relieved when I said that almost everything was going straight into the basement.

The friends that Stephen had just picked up at the airport, however, were an entirely different matter. Of course, people have food they don't enjoy or even can't possibly eat. For Stephen it's liver, and please don't offer me tripe or anything animally that too closely resembles the original. Outside of that, we can manage it all with a smile.

'Hi, had a good siesta? Just doing us a bit of supper. Oh, I forgot to ask, is there anything that you two don't eat?'

'Tomatoes, onions and garlic, and Damien hates all fish.'

I don't know who was more pissed off: me or the paella simmering on the hob.

9

Four Cats and a Funeral

Stephen's darling Uncle Jack died that first June, and we went back to Britain for the funeral. Three days later, arriving home at our sleepy La Molineta in the early evening, we were surprised to see at least a dozen people wandering around in the road.

A cat with her three kittens had been living in the hay barn very happily; we had seen them several times, and her babies were about four or five weeks old. I often took milk to the very shy young mum, who seemed little more than a kitten herself. She always ignored it until she thought I had gone, then wolfed the lot. For reasons obviously known only to her, she had decided to move her babies. She had crossed the road once and successfully deposited a kitten in the bushes on the other side, but had been hit by a car when trying to move kitten number two. She was dead, and Antonio was dealing with that side of things. Everyone else was on a kitten hunt. The little mite she had had in her mouth at the time had shot under the bonnet of Mayte's French husband, Roger's, car; his solution to this, which I thought a tad drastic, was to start the engine. It worked, though, and a tiny black-and-white bundle was quickly stuffed into a cardboard box. It was easy to find the second baby in the bushes and, in theory, the remaining kitten, still in the haystack, would not be a problem. She had other ideas, though, and when uncovered shot up the nearest drainpipe and refused to be moved. A plate of tuna, a saucer of milk, lots of 'puss puss puss, clever girl, pretty girl'. Nothing.

We were, once again, back to the Roger school of cat rescue. He turned his hose on full blast and shoved it up the pipe. The kitten, now known as Pantoja, appeared with a woosh. Tiny to begin with – the smallest of the three – and soaking wet, she was a pathetic sight. Mission accomplished. A drink in Antonio's seemed essential and everyone congratulated everyone else on a job well done. For a full hour, I must confess, the kittens in their cardboard box were forgotten. We were all leaving when Antonio shoved the box at me.

'For you.'

'No, Antonio. No.'

'You love animals.'

'Yes, you know I do. But we have a puppy now.'

'True. Keep for tonight. Tomorrow I will sort it.'

And that is how we came to be the proud owners of Pavarotti, Picasso and Pantoja, or, rather, as is almost always the case with cats, how they came to own us. To name Picasso was easy: he was the black-and-white one with an off-centre stripe down his nose. The other two would have fooled any breeder of Siamese seal points, even down to the knobbly lumps on the ends of their tails. One was fat and, with the previous *P* in mind, he became Pavarotti. His almost identical but skinnier little sister sang all the time, actually more of a trill than a song. Here there is a famous lady singer, Isabel Pantoja, whose husband was a bullfighter who died in the ring, leaving her with a baby daughter. She would appear on stage with her little girl, both dressed in matching flamenco dresses, and sing love songs to her dead husband. The Spanish love a good sob story; every song she released went straight to number one. So our little singer is La Pantoja, aka Issy. Not a Mediterranean tabby in sight.

We installed them in the little bedroom off the kitchen for the first night. They had a saucer of milk and a plate of ham for midnight snacks, and a fluffy turquoise towel that really brought out the blue in their eyes. I left the bedside light on in case they got scared. Charly's nose went into overdrive; we obviously smelled different and very interesting. It didn't even cross our minds that cats and dogs are not supposed to get on. The following morning when I opened the bedroom door, they rushed into a huddle in the corner, with wide eyes as round as Polo Mints. As I slowly moved towards them, Picasso pulled himself up to his full four inches, added another inch by bristling the spiky fur across his back and danced towards me sideways on all four paws.

'Hello, babies, I'm your new mum.'

As I bent down to scoop up Picasso, he took a big breath and spat at me. I fled.

'The black-and-white one spat at me.'

'What did you do?'

'Nothing. I just said I was their new mum.'

'That would explain it.'

We left the bedroom door open, and over the course of the next hour, they edged towards the kitchen. Picasso was the first to approach Charly. Again adopting the feline Rudolf Nureyev approach, he danced to within a foot of Charly's nose, then reversed gear and executed a moonwalk, returning to his siblings with a look of triumph. Charly didn't flinch. The pantomime continued throughout the day, but animals adapt easily, especially very young ones, and by that evening we were one big happy family.

Lourdes

When we bought La Panificadora and agreed to honour the rental contract until the end of October, we inherited Adora. Adora had looked after the house for more than 20 years and fulfilled the specified 'maid service twice weekly' clause in the contract. She saw this change of ownership as her time to retire, but did promise to find us a new cleaner. As promised, the following Wednesday, Adora arrived to clean La Panificadora with Lourdes, her second cousin's sister-in-law's nephew's best friend's wife, or some such village connection. They did a brilliant job. Stephen maintains that Frigiliana is the world academy of cleaners. Two hours later, Adora reported that Lourdes understood what was required and that she would be our cleaner from now on. Lourdes Martín Martín. (Here you keep your father's name when you marry and acquire your husband's as your second. Rather posh, really; everyone is always double-barrelled. Her parents are first cousins, hence Martín Martín.) She smiled shyly and they left.

On Saturday, her next work day, she was sitting at the bottom of our steps at quarter to ten.

'Hello Lourdes. You're early.'

'Yes. Sorry, I thought I might not get a lift, but I was lucky. Sorry.'

'It is not a problem. You were going to walk here from the village?'

'Of course.'

'Come in, have a coffee.'

We talked for a few minutes. Looking back, it now seems hard to believe that the enormous character that is Lourdes was at the time so timid. I learned that her husband, Julio, was the local goat man, with a flock of three hundred, and, at the time, though now long-eaten, they also had two piglets named Serrano and Iberico, after the hams! She had left school at 14 (normal for the time), helped her mother at home until she married at 18 and had her son the following year. Lourdes is the middle one of three sisters and the mother of one boy, also a Julio. It is traditional here that the first-born son is named after the father, and the same applies to mothers and daughters (although all that is changing rapidly and there are probably more newborn Brooklyns and Kylies in the village these days than Plácidos or Inmaculadas). Years later, she would explain how excited, delighted and terrified she was during those first few weeks working for us. This, her first job, meant her first taste of independence, the first few pesetas she was going to earn and, more importantly, the first that she could choose how to spend.

She is a five-feet-by-three-feet Lycra-clad bubbly dynamo; reverse these numbers and you get her age. Her chipped and ragged fingernails were always painted a lurid pink, purple or, occasionally, blue. Quite pale-skinned for an Andalucían *campo* wife, she turns crimson for a week in early spring and is mahogany by mid-June, although this tan, so coveted by holidaymakers, never quite disguises the bites and scratches on her arms and legs that come from working with three hundred goats. She has cheap gold rings on every finger, some of which have been there for so long that, like the bindings on young trees, the skin has begun to grow around them. Five thin gold chains adorn her neck. One of these bears the inscription 'Lrods', a present from her aunt and uncle at her baptism before they had learned to read or write. She has a passion for high heels and handbags, and hair colours, too; since earning her own spending money, she has been every shade from peroxide blonde to almost black. After a recent disastrous trip to the hairdresser – who is, of course, a cousin – she arrived home bright orange, causing Julio to rave at her for spending good money to look like a gas bottle. Her stamina is as spectacular as her voice; she works like a demon and sings like an angel.

When David, my grown-up son, first came back to visit, having spent his childhood summers here, he was just beginning to really enjoy Spanish music.

'I wouldn't mind a copy of this one.'

'Copy of what?'

'I don't know who she is, but she's got a great voice.'

'You can't copy that; it's Lourdes singing along to the radio.'

Lourdes may never have worked before, but she certainly knew how to clean. Of course, the climate helps. It is possible to douse almost everything in copious amounts of water, pop it outside for ten minutes and it is dry. This approach she applied to everything: mattresses, sofa cushions and rugs. Even though Charly learned very early in life that when Lourdes was in the house to stand still was to be in imminent danger of being washed, he adored her, and the feeling was mutual.

In those early days, with only one young dog and three small kittens in the house, she would clean for us for four hours a week and then go next door to La Panificadora mid-week and on Saturdays when people were arriving and leaving to do a thorough blitz. To begin with, she was very nervous about entering The Pan, especially if there were clients lying by the pool, but she quickly picked up 'good moaning, I am your cleaner' and felt much more comfortable once she was able to introduce herself. We all settled into this routine.

One Saturday morning a couple of months or so later, soon after the latest clients had left, Lourdes, as usual, had gone next door to start work. Within seconds, she was back.

'Jackie, there is a letter here with my name, then some English writing and some money.'

'Lourdes, it is for you, it says thank you for looking after them. *Es un consejo*.' I had got it wrong again. The only word I knew for a tip was *consejo*, which actually means 'advice', as in how to do something – 'I'll give you a tip.' I should have used *propina* (a gratuity).

She started crying.

'Why are you crying, Lourdes?'

'Before this the people did not leave money. Do all the people who were here before think that I did *not* look after them, and did these people think I need money for lessons in how to clean?'

Some tip, some don't, and I got the words wrong. Try explaining that with only basic Spanish.

II

La Panificadora

At the end of October, the rental contract expired and with it my frustrations of that summer. Casa Rosa didn't have a pool at the time, and a summer spent listening to the delighted squeals and splashes coming from people next door in *my* pool as the temperature hit the high nineties was, shall we say, not easy.

Only having access to the house every other Saturday for four hours, I would rush in with my tape measure and paint charts as soon as the latest tenants had loaded their cars. Now it was ours, really ours.

The month that Paco promised it would take to strip and rebuild the kitchen turned out to be almost two, something that should have taught us a lesson for the future but didn't at the time. So, on 21 December, the day before eight friends and family arrived for Christmas, Lourdes and I were busy dragging crates up from the basement and unpacking long-forgotten treasures. Stephen arrived in the kitchen just as Lourdes was exclaiming that she was surprised at how many of the casserole dishes, pots, plates and jugs were exactly like the ones from around here; she had thought they would have been different, having come from England. He rolled his eyes, grunted and left. For more than ten years, we had never left Spain without armfuls of pottery, sometimes paying excess baggage for the privilege. Now we had paid again to bring them all home.

Home. Home. *Home*. At last I was home. My father was a lifetime army man with the Royal Scots; it meant that we had moved a lot. In fact, we moved from Penicuik to Colchester in the ten days around my birth. Ten days, the time spent in hospital in those days to '*dar luz*' (to give light), the Spanish expression for giving birth. My mother waddled out of one house in southern Scotland and carried me back into another in southern England. It set a pattern that seemed like it would continue for the rest of my life.

Now was going to be so different, so permanent. La Panificadora, with its walled and terraced gardens, trickling water, arches and mill stones, views of sea and mountains; its newly designed kitchen, for me the perfect blend of modern appliances hidden behind rustic doors, and with tons of space for friends to sit and chat while we cooked. I would never, ever move again.

I felt more settled than I ever had in my life, but the animals were confused. Moving next door was a doddle for us, but they could not grasp the concept. Charly always beat us home after our walks; he would race the last few hundred yards up the track and sit at the top of Casa Rosa's steps waiting for us. This took a long time to change. 'Wrong house, Charly,' didn't work; it was only when we walked past him and up the stairs of La Panificadora that he would grudgingly follow. He shunned his wicker basket for the first month after the move, preferring to lie across the front door, but he did accept that his food bowl had miraculously moved and didn't lose his appetite. We thought it would be easier for the cats, but it wasn't. Ever since they had been old enough to climb the garden wall, they had spent a lot of time running between the two houses. Luckily, the various people who rented Casa Rosa in those first few months were animal lovers, too. One lady who had put her cat into a cattery for the holiday was delighted that a beautiful big Siamese slept at the bottom of her bed every night.

12

Charly Grows Up

We revelled in the luxury of lie-ins, me in particular, and unless we had builders arriving, 9 a.m. would often find us sipping coffee, sitting on the terrace still wrapped in towelling robes and planning the day ahead. Charly was a good dog, something that we told him often and that he always seemed pleased to hear.

Stephen had searched for dog-training books on his first trip back to London and, being in a rush as usual, had gone for two extremes. One advised that man was the master and that the puppy had to learn this at an early stage. It also had lots of instructions about using rolled-up newspapers to practically beat the poor thing into submission and cages to keep it confined. The other was all about never saying 'no' and recommended that every animal deserved to have the time and space to find and express its own personality. Saying 'no' may restrict its ability to 'project itself'. Charly was my first dog but not my first child, and in child-rearing I had found that 'no' was a very useful word. On the other hand, though, I had never used a rolled-up newspaper or a cage – actually, I suppose that is not strictly true because David did have a playpen. Anyway, both books went in the rubbish bin and we just followed our instincts.

For months, either one of us had been walking Charly first thing every morning to the top of the track that led down to the river. He would then run off, do what he had to do and be sitting outside our door waiting to be let in within ten or fifteen minutes. One Sunday, he didn't return. After two hours, Stephen walked down to the river-bed, but there was no sign of him. After four hours, Stephen drove around looking for him. Nothing. I walked halfway back down the rough track to the river and stopped at José and Adela's house to ask if they had seen him. Although we didn't know them well at this stage, they would always smile and wave as we passed. Not only had Adela not seen Charly, but her little dog, Bobby, a pal of Charly's, had also gone out that morning and not returned. Stephen and I went to bed late that night, reassuring each other that he was bound to be fine, that he had probably just got distracted by an interesting smell. We both got up several times when we thought the other was asleep to see whether he was sitting on our steps. He wasn't.

Late the next morning, Adela knocked on our door in floods of tears with an incredible story. In town that morning, she had been stopped in the street by a woman she didn't know who told her that both Charly and her little Bobby had been stolen. They were being kept in a basement in Calle Granada, one of the smartest residential streets in Nerja, by foreigners who were going to take Bobby back to France for medical experiments. But they had decided that they didn't want Charly and were going to kill him before they left. She said the woman then ran off before she could stop her. We couldn't make sense of what we were hearing. It just seemed so far-fetched, but by the time she had finished I too was crying. That evening, Stephen went to see Adela's husband, José, to suggest that they both go and knock on every door in Calle Granada to try to find foreigners that might be living there and might have a basement. José, looking very embarrassed, told Stephen that he was sure they would be wasting their time, just as Adela had already wasted their money. The truth was that she had not been stopped in the street, as she said, but she had been too embarrassed to

admit that she had gone to the local *adivina* (white witch) and
paid her to tell what had happened to the dogs by reading the
cards. We were both astounded and relieved. But Charly was
still missing.

For the following five days, our lives were ruled by Charly's
absence. Was he injured, dead? Was he lost and confused and
walking further away from us every day? Armed with a photo,
Stephen toured the myriad tracks around here for hours at a
time, stopping to ask anyone and everyone if they had seen
him. I wouldn't leave the house in case there was any news.
Looking back now, those five days were probably the only time
that we have felt isolated and slightly at odds with people here.
Our friends, both English and Spanish, were supportive and
sympathetic, but our mission brought us into contact with
many of the older men who had spent their lives scraping a
living from a hostile patch of land. They showed interest in the
photograph for only one reason: they were stunned that anyone
would waste a photo on their dog. They were never rude; we
were often offered first pick of the next litter of puppies that
their dog was bound to have. These men, who had been young
boys when civil war ravaged their already struggling country,
had no understanding of our feelings. In those relatively early
days of our new lives, I thought their attitude was heartless; it
took much longer to fully understand their reasoning, though
it is not a view I can ever share.

By the following Friday, with little hope, we set off yet again.
After four hours, and at least five miles from home, we called it
a day. Minutes later, Stephen was driving and I was still hanging
out of the side window calling Charly's name in a voice that by
this time was almost hoarse.

'Charly, there you are.'

'Stephen, don't joke. This is not bloody funny.'

Then I looked ahead. Lying by the side of the road a few
yards in front of us were two exhausted dogs, both filthy. It took

me a few seconds to realise that one of them was ours, then I was out of the car before it had stopped.

The ugly bitch that had tempted him away (of course I am only using the correct term for a female dog here) was, in truth, one of the ugliest bitches I had ever seen. As instructed, Charly got into the car, although he looked less than delighted to see us, and in a moment of madness, Stephen suggested that we take the girlfriend, too.

'Are you insane?'

'Well, she's probably going to have Charly's puppies.'

'Exactly. In fact, she's almost definitely going to have Charly's puppies. Just drive, please, just drive.'

We took him home and he walked up the steps like John Wayne. We hosed him down, removed at least a dozen ticks, covered him in flea powder and gave him a lecture about safe sex and his poor taste in women. He ate, lots, then went to his basket and slept for 48 hours with a big smile on his face. I cried with relief, and Stephen was grinning like an idiot. Luckily the canine version of the Child Support Agency has never caught up with us. Bobby, José and Adela's little dog, found his own way home safely later that same day.

13

Sybil and Blas

Sybil lived above us in a charming little cottage, El Huerto (The Orchard), with a beautiful garden reached by about 50 yards of steep dirt track. She was in her late eighties when we first met. One of the first women to go to Cambridge, she then went into the diplomatic service, had travelled the world and was still prone to wonderful remarks such as: 'Darling, Moscow in the '30s was a hoot. We were starving, of course, but vodka cost peanuts.'

She was apparently married for a short time in her late twenties, but dismissed it as 'a state that didn't agree with me'. Two black-and-white photographs and an oil painting in her living room proved the fact that she was a stunner in her day. She was 'at home' between four and five thirty every weekday and always dressed for the occasion in slightly faded, carefully darned cashmere twinsets, pearls, a smudge of pale-pink lipstick, baby-blue eyeshadow and a splash of Chanel No 5. She would then sit on her terrace and watch for anyone coming up the track, although we never saw anyone else visit.

She died before we moved here permanently, but while on holiday I would visit her almost every day and often do her shopping. Once, she had batteries on her shopping list, batteries for the little radio beside her bed, though when I replaced the old with the new I could not tune it. Most efficiently, she found the faded instruction manual, and, deciding that it was definitely a 'boy thing', I went to find Stephen.

'Sybil says she only needs three channels: the local radio, Madrid Classical and the BBC World Service.'

'OK. Won't take a minute.'

After almost two hours of much muttering and swearing, the radio was finally programmed. It was, of course, the fault of the badly translated Japanese manual that it had taken so long!

'Right, here we go; I've written it down for Sybil. Button One: local radio; Button Two: Madrid Classical; and the BBC World Service is on Three.'

'Sybil, sorry it took so long, but here we are. Stephen has written it all down for you, look.'

She looked at the piece of paper, and then: 'Well, thank you my dear girl, but it's not possible that the BBC is on Three; it has always been on One.'

'Well, it's on Button Three now, Sybil, and your other two stations are on One and Two.'

'Bloody BBC! They have changed their wavelength without telling anyone: it's appalling, it's a scandal. I know the Director General, had cocktails with him on many an occasion, I shall write immediately. I probably didn't even need new batteries.'

No amount of persuasion would convince her that this was not the case; in the end, I gave up and left her rummaging through drawers to find the address she was looking for.

Sybil had a long-running feud with Blas, the man who tended the sluice gates of the *acequia*. She made it very clear to poor Blas that she did not find his shouts acceptable. Lourdes had been working for us for at least a year before we found out he was her father.

He had retired by then; many years of standing at strange angles, of twisting, turning and tugging, had taken their toll on his back and his knees. But to have retired did not mean to be idle. He filled his days with three major activities. Ensuring that the family, his wife, three daughters and their assorted offspring, lived a frugal life took up a lot of his time and a lot of their patience. Early evenings found him sitting on a low wall at the entrance to the village, one of the flock of aged sparrows, chins supported by canes as they watched their ever-changing world go by. Also, he still worked hard on his land, producing sweet onions, tiny earthy potatoes and tomatoes that oozed juice.

One Christmas the girls, Aurora, Lourdes and Carmina, pooled their present money to buy a new light fitting for their parents. For months, their mother's much-prized needlework had suffered as her eyesight began to fail, and the one overhead bulb in their living room provided inadequate light to almost invisibly darn favourite clothes.

The girls bought them a chandelier. Eight gold tulips, each bearing a sixty-watt bulb, were offered to the ceiling by gold arms strung with glass beads. The sisters made complicated arrangements to keep Blas and his wife, Aurora, out of the house while the sons-in-law installed the lamp. Mama was delighted. Blas was impressed by the amount of light it was possible to achieve in one room; to him, it was like being at *feria*, the annual three-day village festival that throbs with sound and pulses with light.

The chandelier still dominates the room today, but, within two days of its installation, with the help of a rickety old stool, Blas removed seven of the bulbs. He thanked his daughters and said that now he probably would not need to buy another bulb for the rest of his life.

14

Domingo

I still don't know where time goes here; now the years skip by. That first March till Christmas just disappeared. Charly grew in many ways, as you have heard. Apart, that is, from his ears, which have never changed from the day we got him. To begin with they hung to his chin, looking promisingly like those of a pointer, but over the months, as his head got bigger the ears didn't, and instead they became small flyaway afterthoughts on the side. He dug a hole in the garden, a hole at least a foot deep, between the roots of the jacaranda tree, and on the rare occasions that he was in trouble, he would go and sit in it, hiding his head between his paws. We called this hole his 'Trophy Cupboard'. We always knew where to find anything that went missing: shoes, books, pens, tea towels . . . He was particularly fond of my bras: never chewed, just saved in Charly's Trophy Cupboard.

We were beginning to take for granted the fact that we woke to sunshine every morning. Unless we were going out, shorts, shirts and flip-flops were all that were necessary. One morning in the second week of November – I remember the date well: the eleventh, it was Stephen's birthday – Charly started barking loudly. This was unusual. He never was, and, indeed, still isn't, a very vocal dog. His preferred style of communication is usually a sort of short chuff that makes the wobbly bits at the side of his mouth, well, wobble. The barking continued, and we went

to investigate. He was standing in the middle of the terrace, and
it had started to rain big, slow, fat plops that splashed onto the
sun-baked terracotta tiles and spread mysteriously. He pawed at
the tiles as he would an insect, but was driven indoors when a
drop landed on his nose. It took us a moment to realise that, like
us, he had taken the sunshine for granted, though, unlike us, he
was too young to remember the last time it had rained.

Of course, had the opportunity to acquire a Spanish pointer
arisen, we would certainly have been very tempted, but with
three cats, the idea of Mediterranean tabbies was most definitely
on the back burner. In fact, we had decided that one dog was
enough. He came everywhere with us; he was trained to sit, to
stay and not to touch food without our permission.

On 4 January, with Charly at our side, we went to Antonio's
for a drink. Here, the early days of January are a bit of time in
limbo. Christmas officially starts on 8 December, with the Feast
of the Immaculate Conception. I was brought up in a typical
Catholic family and, when old enough to notice such things, I
was always very impressed that Mary had only been pregnant
for 17 days. There must be a God. It seemed to take normal
women, and even my rabbit, much longer than that.

Christmas Eve, Nochebuena, is celebrated with a big family
meal after the Midnight Mass, and the party continues until
dawn. There is an old Spanish saying: *esta noche es Nochebuena,
y no es noche de dormir* (this is the good night and not the night
for sleep). Christmas Day is a time for church services, religious
reflection and the nursing of hangovers.

There are big parties in the Plaza de la Iglesia on New Year's
Eve, when, according to village tradition, it is very important that
the women wear red knickers to ensure luck in the coming year.
Nobody has been able to even begin to explain why, although I
suspect it is linked to fertility. Then, as the church clock chimes
midnight, everyone tries to eat 12 grapes before the last chime,
which is a lot more difficult than it sounds.

The New Year's Eve of 1998, going into 1999, certainly had links to fertility in Frigiliana. The electricity had been going on and off all evening, but just after eleven it packed up for the night. The celebrations in the plaza were cancelled, the bars and restaurants closed and, although dressed in their finest and ready for a long party, everyone went home. For weeks, people bemoaned the fact that it had been one of the least celebrated new years that they could remember. Five or six months later, however, it became very apparent that private celebrations had continued: the following late September and early October, twenty-two babies were born. When they started school three years later, it was the first time in the history of the village that there were two entry classes.

The present-giving that we associate with Christmas Day is not until 6 January: Día de los Reyes (the Day of the Kings). It is only the greed of our modern society that celebrates the birth of Christ with presents on 25 December. On the night of 5 January, all the children in the village put their shoes on their doorsteps, filled with carrots and straw for the three kings' horses, and are rewarded with presents the following day. Consequently, although there are probably ten Spanish working days from early December till mid-January, none of them are really taken very seriously. It is one very long holiday.

So, on 4 January, once again we took the 60-second walk to Antonio's, and the bar was full of 'workers' on their way home. Rosario, still firmly ensconced in our basement every night, is, of course, accepted in the bar as the wife of Antonio.

Female foreigners, after walking in the mountains, stop for drinks and that has now become the norm. But for a local woman, even if she is not Spanish and is also accompanied by her husband, the etiquette is to sit with Rosario quietly in a corner. So, sitting quietly in the corner talking to Rosario, I watched as Plácido arrived on his battered old scooter and ordered his usual *vino de terreno*, the local sweet Málaga wine that had caused me so much damage on the night that I had offered to sort out the puppy problem, some nine months before. I haven't touched it since. I listened with half an ear to the background conversation, while enjoying Rosario's tales; she was full of stories of her recent biannual trip to Málaga. At the bar, Plácido was animatedly talking to Antonio.

'I'll be back, I just need to get rid of this . . . I don't suppose you need a new dog, do you, Antonio?'

'What do you think?'

'No. OK. I'll be back in a minute.'

Stephen stopped Plácido on his way out of the bar and asked to look at the dog. From his inside jacket pocket, Plácido lifted a tiny puppy and passed it over to Stephen. It sat in the palm of his hand.

'He would have been a good dog, from this mother they always have been; she always has good dogs. But he is the smallest of the three, and she is old now; this is her seventh litter. She has little milk these days and can only just manage to feed two.'

'So what are you going to do with him?'

'Put him down the *acequia*.'

'Drown him?'

'What else? No one will take him. What else can I do? It will be a quicker, kinder death than starving.'

I could hear it coming.

'*Jackie.*'

It was a Sunday. We took him from a gentle, kind man who deserved his name, Plácido, and by then we already had a cat called Pavarotti. This dog had to be a Domingo. We assured each other that one more very small dog wouldn't make any difference; like children, two can in fact at times be less trouble than one, and such good company for each other. I tucked him inside my coat. He grunted, peed and fell asleep.

Domingo. Our second dog to be introduced to the vet. Again it was Rafael, professional, polite; yet, when working, short on charm to humans, but full of love for animals. He went through the usual checks. Then:

'You have children?'

'I have a son, yes, but he is grown up now.'

'Good. But still you remember four-hourly feeds?'

'God, yes.'

'Good. You feed this every four hours for the next month or he will most certainly die. He is probably not yet three weeks old, but, if looked after, he should grow up to be healthy.'

I stifled the temptation to rush out and buy blue Babygros and a wicker crib, and instead set about the less romantic and more practical task of bottle-feeding a very tiny puppy. He would not eat. He gagged on the teat and threw his head from side to side with impressive force, but he grew weaker by the hour. In desperation, just before midnight, I called and woke my mum in England. She was born and raised on a farm and was of the 'no-nonsense' school.

'Cut your little fingernail as short as you possibly can. I am presuming here that your nails are as ridiculous as ever?'

'They are sort of longish.'

'Exactly. Cut it off, file it smooth, then try and put your finger as flat as possible into some warm milk, with just the tip above the milk, and encourage him to suck it. Wring out a warm, wet flannel and stroke the back of his head with this at the same time; it replicates the mother's tongue. Oh, and wrap a small clock in a towel and put it beside him when you put him down to sleep; he'll think it's his mother's heartbeat. Call back tonight if you have a problem, I'll sleep on the settee in case you do. Good luck, darling.'

It worked. Amazingly, within a minute or two he didn't even need my little finger; he had learned to lap and wanted more and more warm milk, so much so that as it was going in at one end, it began to come out at the other. It was a huge relief, but not the end of the road. It was still party season, and Spanish

parties never last for fewer than four hours. He had to come
with us. I dug out an old esparto-grass bag with long leather
handles – the type the local women use for carrying vegetables
back from the market – and, in my party finery, slung this over
my shoulder wherever we went. Inside, swaddled in a towel,
lying on a hot-water bottle, was our little Domingo. The bars
of the village, always very accommodating to people with young
children, were surprised, amused and helpful. He thrived and
soon grew into one of those dogs we swore we would never have:
the typical short, stocky Andalucían village dog whose tail curls
over his back. He was good with the cats – it helped that they
were much bigger than him for the first few months; in fact,
Pavarotti still is – although, at times, he could be a little over-
enthusiastic. I have often wondered what the people holidaying
next door in Casa Rosa thought of my plea: 'Domingo, how
many times have I told you – don't do that to Pavarotti.'

It wasn't long until we could take away the brick ramps we
had put on the steep garden steps to help him, with his stumpy
little legs, to follow Charly everywhere. They were, and, indeed,
still are, inseparable.

15

Water Slides

Unlike Charly, it was probably a good six weeks before Domingo had his first proper car journey. They were both in the back of the car on the way to their walk on the beach. Quite understandably, most of the beaches around here have now banned dogs, but there are still a few, off the beaten track, where it is possible to let them run, and they love it. Stephen was driving, and I was looking over my shoulder and laughing at the way that the little one was trying to copy Charly. With his back legs on the armrest, he was at full stretch to get his nose out of the back window, which was about a third open.

'He's safe, isn't he? I mean, he couldn't fall out.'

'Of course not; don't worry, he's fine.'

Reassured, I turned round again to check on the two dogs in the back seat.

'*Stop the car!*'

'What?'

'Domingo's gone! He's not here!'

'Don't be stupid.'

Stephen pulled over, and we searched the Land Rover in vain. He was not there.

With impressive speed, I became hysterical. With impressive calm, Stephen took charge. I was to walk back to where we had last seen him in the car, two, certainly no more than three minutes before. He would drive. And so it was that I came to be running up and down the Spanish version of a country lane on a Saturday evening in early spring shouting, 'Domingo, Domingo'. *Domingo* in Spanish means Sunday. Is it surprising the locals think we're all mad? I did two laps on foot, calling out to the men working in the fields, asking if they had found a puppy with a red collar, and expecting at any minute to find a little beige splat of a pancake on the road.

We swapped: I drove, and Stephen took Charly on his lead and walked the same route. The theory was that Charly would be keen and useful in trying to find his little brother. The reality was that Charly enjoyed the walk and showed no interest or concern for Domingo. On lap three, an old man waved me down.

'I've got your puppy; I've put him in the back of my van.'

'Is he all right?'

'Yes, he's fine. He was in the *acequia*, but if it wasn't for the sluice gate he would be in the Mediterranean by now and on his way to Africa.'

Domingo was fine: soggy, but fine. With odds of millions to one, he must have fallen from the car window straight into the water channel. The water is quite shallow but fast-running, and the sides of the *acequia* are steep. He had travelled for at least a mile. Thoughts of a walk on the beach were long gone; we went home, dried him off and had a therapeutic brandy.

16

The Honourable Pig

The following Sunday, we were invited to Antonio's house for lunch. His sons, Antonio and Paco, and their sister, María, were all going to be there with their families; it was to be a big event. We accepted with pleasure, until . . .

'Jackie, I am killing the pig in your honour.'

'The pig? You're killing it?'

'Yes. In your honour.'

'Antonio, no. No, it's a lovely pink pig, thank you very much, but I would be much more honoured if it lived.'

He thought this a good joke.

At nine on Sunday morning, he banged on the door. There is no mistaking Antonio's knock. He ignores the beautiful closed hand of Fatima and instead prefers the gnarled one of Antonio. Stephen answered in his dressing gown.

'That was Antonio. The butcher has arrived and is ready to kill the pig.'

'Oh, how sad.'

'They are waiting for you.'

'Me? Why?'

'Because it's being killed in your honour.'

'We've been through all this; you know how I hate it.'

'Tough, they're waiting for you.'

'Make an excuse. I'm ill or something.'

'No.'

I summoned up my best look. Thank God it worked, and Stephen padded off to make my excuses, assuring Antonio that I would be fine very soon and we would be there by two at the latest.

Rosario's house (for the bar is Antonio's and the house Rosario's) is always a delight. She begs, borrows and, yes, probably acquires plant cuttings from everyone around here, and uses old olive-oil cans and paint drums as flowerpots. The result is a picturesque Spanish version of Steptoe's yard. Built on the steep hillside, the only token gestures to safety are the many old doors and bed bases stacked up at the edge of the kitchen that stop you falling a good 50 feet into the avocado trees below. Inside the tiny house, there are many statues to Jesus and the Virgin. Vases are laden with plastic roses with plastic water drops on their petals, hand-crocheted antimacassars adorn every chair and similar mats on every surface are topped by much-prized official photos of christenings, first communions and weddings. It is only possible to navigate that living room with a sideways step.

We arrived just before two at a scene from *The Texas Chainsaw Massacre*. There were bits of pig everywhere. The women – Rosario, her daughter, María, and her two daughters-in-law – were scraping bits of meat from skin and bone, mixing the result with lots of paprika, chopped garlic, handfuls of stale breadcrumbs and then stuffing it into the intestines to make chorizo sausage. I now understand the origin of the expression 'up to your arms in it'.

My honourable pink pig was skinned and pinned to a door by its forelegs; actually, his pose rather resembled some of the statues inside the house. Miss this next bit if, like me, you are squeamish. I closed my eyes when I typed it.

The butcher was carving great slabs of meat from the haunches and passing them to Paco, who was layering them in huge rubber buckets and throwing handfuls of salt between each layer. The old washing-up bowl underneath caught most of the blood, which was saved to make *morcilla*, a spicy version of black pudding. But the bowl didn't catch it all, and I noticed that when Rosario got up to fetch more bread her cheap foam slippers left squelchy bloody footprints in her wake. When a bucket was full, it was topped off with olive oil and wrestled down to the cool storeroom under the house. This was to be the whole family's meat for the coming year.

Family friends, mostly old men, had turned the activities into a spectator sport. They were focusing on the trotters, brain, ears and tongue, having a heated argument about the preferred method of preservation of such delicacies. Meanwhile, the makeshift barbecue, a piece of corrugated iron on some bricks, began to glow. The griddle was brushed with olive oil and sprigs of rosemary were shoved between the burning pine logs. Wafer-thin slices of pork began to sizzle and spit, crusty bread was cut, red local wine was poured and – in my honour – I was offered the first piece of meat.

I turned my back to the family and looked frantically at Stephen.

'I can't do this.'

'Course you can.'

'Can't.'

'You have to. Turn round, face everyone, big smile, big bite, OK.'

'OK.'

I turned, faced everyone, big smile, about to take a big bite. The butcher chose that exact moment to decapitate the pig. Luckily, Stephen caught me.

17

San Sebastian and San Antonio

Contrary to popular belief, most Spaniards do work as hard as they play, although there always seems to be the time and a reason or excuse for a party. As I said, Christmas isn't over until 6 January. Then, on the 20th, comes the fiesta of San Sebastian, the patron saint of Frigiliana – actually one of the village's two, but he is the original. With his day being in January, the weather cannot be guaranteed: not good news for the parades and picnics that accompany a saint's day. So early last century, the village simply adopted San Antonio, whose day is 13 June and much more likely to promise – in fact, almost guarantee – good weather. Thus probably two-thirds of the village men are called Antonio and many of the rest are Sebastian.

On 20 January, San Sebastian is decked with flowers, taken out of the church and, following Mass, carried around the village on the men's shoulders as the sun sets. To carry the saint is an honour and a right passed from father to son, or, if necessary, from uncle to nephew. The fiesta is a relatively subdued affair; people are still recovering from the excesses of Christmas, and I always think of Sebastian as our second-class saint.

The fiesta of San Antonio, on the other hand, is the village's biggest annual event. Our house is beside the road that leads up to the village from the coast: the only road; everything on its way to Frigiliana passes our kitchen window. The first attraction arrives about a week before the 13th: the funfair, a charmingly old-fashioned collection of dodgems, coconut shies, bouncy castles and trampolines. There are shooting galleries, house-of-horror rides and the test-your-strength machines so very popular with spotty teenage boys trying to show off to the gaggles of giggling young girls. Food stalls offer the usual hot dogs and hamburgers along with the more traditional fiesta food of spit-roast chicken. At the end of the night, at around five or six in the morning, many revellers need a sugar fix, and it is time for *churros* and hot chocolate. *Churros* are squiggles of a doughnut-like batter squeezed from a fat-nozzled icing tube into a bubbling cauldron of spitting oil. Served in a poke, like chips, they are sprinkled with sugar and washed down with thick, strong, dark hot chocolate. If you find it a bit rich, you could slap it directly onto your hips and thighs, achieving the same end result but without the enjoyment.

By mid-June, the night-time temperature is often in the high seventies, so nothing gets going until well after ten in the evening. Then the whole village, dressed in their Sunday best, start to arrive. Three, sometimes four, generations of one family will promenade through the streets stopping to chat with friends and watch the fun.

On the first night there is the annual Miss Frigiliana competition, open to all the village girls who have their sixteenth birthday that year, which attracts an average of ten to twelve entrants. Billed to start at ten, it sometimes manages to get going before midnight. The girls first appear in 'Day Wear', always jeans, white T-shirts emblazoned with the name of their sponsor, Bar Al Andaluz, Frutería Jiménez, and the obligatory platform-soled trainers. This is followed by my favourite, 'Traditional Dress', the beautiful, vibrantly coloured frilly flamenco dresses; the girls wear roses in their hair and have shawls casually draped around bronzed shoulders. Then, finally, 'Evening Wear', turning it into the Miss Jailbait competition. A huge team of local experts is invited to judge this prestigious event: the village hairdresser, the garage owner, last year's winner, the mayor, of course, and several of his councillors.

'Who do you think will win, Lourdes?'

'Well, number seven is really beautiful. Number three is my neighbour's daughter, Miriam, and I know that they spent a fortune on her dress, that would be nice, but I think it will be number eleven.'

'Eleven! No chance.'

'We will see.'

And the winner is . . . number eleven.

'I don't believe it. Who is she, the mayor's daughter?'

'No, no,' said Lourdes, far too quickly, 'the mayor only has sons. Number eleven is his niece.'

On 13 June, we all follow San Antonio down to the river. From nine in the morning, the horses are brought out of the *campo* and begin to trot past our windows on their way up to the village. The men wear black-and-grey striped trousers, white shirts, red cummerbunds and black Córdoban hats. Their horses gleam, their manes and tails plaited with ribbons. In the village, the women, also dressed in the traditional way, join them, seated sidesaddle behind the riders, with the frills of their dresses spread out over the horses' rumps. The flowers in their hair are more than just decoration. They are worn behind your left ear if you are 'available', the right if you are spoken for and on top of your head if you are considered too young for such things. One year I watched with amusement as three girls of about fourteen left their house with their flowers firmly pinned on top of their heads. As they disappeared round the corner, the flowers were swiftly moved to behind their left ears.

After a midday Mass, San Antonio leaves the church, again carried on the shoulders of the men in the village who are honoured to be chosen for the task, and he does a tour of the village before being transferred to an ox cart. He is preceded by the local municipal band, mainly teenagers who break rank at every opportunity and rush into the small crowd to greet their friends, destroying any semblance of solemnity. Then come the riders and the floats. Every conceivable vehicle is decorated with paper chains and palm leaves and has music playing as loud as possible. Scooters, cars, tractors and, more recently, forklifts and dumper trucks (a sign of the times): they all join the procession. In front of all this walks a man with a quiver of rockets slung over one shoulder. Every few minutes he sets one off, startling the horses, making tourists jump and small children and babies cry. The noise is incredible.

Having completed the village tour, this motley procession takes the twisting, almost vertical track that runs from behind the Guardia police station down to the river. The picnic site, in a pinewood, is about a rough two-mile trek upstream. The pink and white oleander are in full bloom, and the smell of pine cones and wild herbs is heady. By June there is little water in the river and many people walk alongside the procession. Cars regularly get stuck and people run to put a shoulder behind them. By about two in the afternoon, most have arrived.

Coolboxes are unpacked and rugs spread under the trees. The elder children are set to work damming the river to provide a paddling pool for the little ones, who, without ceremony, are stripped to their knickers and encouraged to go and play in the water.

Food, as always around here, is a joy to be shared. Andalucía in the days of Franco and before tourism was perhaps the poorest region of Spain. Yet instead of fostering a spirit of 'look out for yourself', it seems that quite the reverse has happened, and never more so than on this day. Families pride themselves on their specialities: Patricia's tortilla; Rosa's *ensalada de tomate y cebolla*; Paco's sardines, skewered onto pine twigs, bathed in sea salt and cooked on an open fire. Not ever daring or presuming to compete with local fare, my eggy-mayo-and-cress sandwiches are now, surprisingly, one of the big hits. So everyone sets out their offerings at their base camp and the parade begins. Essential to this is the *copita*, a sherry-style glass strung on a leather thong worn around the neck. Volume is still on high as people call to each other to come and share a glass or a bite of something. During the course of the afternoon, your *copita* will hold local homemade wine, manzanilla (the very dry, almost salty sherry from Sanlúcar de Barrameda, near Jerez) and, towards the end of the day, brandy. Who says never mix your drinks?

These days, the music traditionally provided by guitars and castanets comes from a local band. Everyone dances. The provision of power to the picnic site has also given rise to a bar set up for just that one day serving ice-cold beer, and a few years ago we even had a giant television screen. That year, on 13 June, Spain were playing Nigeria in the quarter-finals of the World Cup (I'm talking football here), and there was not a man in the village prepared to miss the match to go down to the river. The women rebelled. The beauty of such a small community is that people's actions can, and do, make a difference. A petition was duly drawn up and signed, with over 300 female signatures, and presented to the mayor. It stated quite simply that if the men did not go to the river, nor would the women and children. If nobody went, it would be an insult to San Antonio and a disgrace to the village and to the church for not celebrating the village's saint's day. That is how we ended up with the incongruous sight of a 30-foot television screen, installed and paid for by the town hall, amongst the pine trees.

That year, the women had won the day, but Spain lost the match.

18

Niña

As the nights drew in late that autumn, we called upon yet another Antonio, Antonio de la Lena, the woodman, to bring us our winter firewood. By this time we had tried several sources, but Antonio and his son, also Antonio, provided the best mix: thin slivers of silver-grey almond wood cut and stored from the previous spring and perfect for kindling; pine that gives off a wonderful smoke when burnt and olive, dark and heavy. A dampened olive log will keep the fire burning all night. It was to be our second winter here and our first with the wood-burning stove; it took us a while to get to know it. When we began to feel the warmth of the day fading at around six, we would light the fire. Three hours later, it was doing what it had promised, by which time we were sitting under copious layers of duvets and blankets. If, mid-afternoon, it crosses your mind that you may need a fire that evening, that is the time to light it.

Charly and Domingo were in heaven. Domingo seemed to take a personal interest in selecting the wood: as soon as Stephen picked up the log basket, Domingo was beside him. As the basket was loaded in our basement, he looked on, full of self-importance, sniffing each piece, then watched intently as the fire was laid and lit. I swear that by now if I asked Domingo to pop out and light the fire, he would. He has become known as our fire monitor. Meanwhile, I would lay an old blanket in front of the hearth and that would be the two of them settled for the night.

Late one evening in early December, I was sitting at the table wrapping Christmas presents and feeling rather smug at being so far ahead of the game. The local restaurant had just closed for the evening, it was pouring with rain and a strong, cold east wind – the levanter – was doing its worst. Andalucían houses just aren't designed for cold levanters, with their peculiar way of twisting around buildings and screaming through the smallest gaps in doors and windows.

Above this noise, I thought I heard something else.

'Stephen, there's a funny noise outside.'

'What sort of funny?'

'Don't know, come and listen.'

We listened and peered out of the window but could see nothing, and settled back to our present-wrapping and football-watching. Ten minutes later, I was still swearing that I could hear something above the wind and, knowing me of old, Stephen faced the fact that I was not going to let this drop until he had been out to have a look.

'You were right; there's a dog out here.'

'It must be soaking.'

'Of course it is. It's shivering. I'll bring it in.'

'*No*. Charly and Domingo will go crazy.'

'OK. I'll leave it.'

'*No*.'

'What then?'

'I don't know.'

'We're coming in.'

Bless him, he was soaked, shivering and his hair was plastered to his head. So I gave him a towel and turned my attention to the dog. From that first moment and until this day, she – as she turned out to be – was heartbreakingly grateful for everything we did for her. We dried her in front of the fire, gave her food and clean water, and then just sat talking gently to her. Charly had checked her out the minute she arrived and, nature being what it is, was strutting around the room trying to look like a casual Don Juan, but actually managing more of a clumsy Hugh Grant. Domingo, after the first sniff, went to his basket, put his head under his paws and stayed there till morning.

'Jackie. We don't need another dog: we have two, it's enough.'

'I know, of course it's enough; we can't possibly keep her.'

'She is probably just lost, though she doesn't have a collar.'

'Yes, I'm sure she's just lost. I'll phone Coastline Radio tomorrow, ask if they'll put out a message.'

'Good idea.'

'Sweet, isn't she?'

'We can't have another dog.'

'I know, we have agreed that. Sweet, isn't she?'

I did phone the radio station and they did put out an appeal. Even better than that, I told Lourdes to ask around in the village, achieving much more coverage than local radio. I asked all the neighbours; the people running the restaurant said they had been feeding her with scraps for more than a week. While we were waiting for her owners to turn up, it seemed only wise to make our next visit to Rafael. After all, I argued, we didn't want our two catching anything that she might have, and while there, it seemed silly not to take advantage of their special Christmas offer on dog baskets; she had been sleeping on an old towel for almost three weeks.

The night that we took her in and discovered she was a she, I started to refer to her as Niña. It means 'little girl' and was, of course, only a temporary name. Yet Niña she is. The closest I can come to pinpointing a breed is her passing resemblance to a golden spaniel. She has partially webbed feet, no tail (naturally; it hasn't been docked) and loves water – all water. Weeks later, Stephen was again watching football and I was soaking in a very expensive bubble bath, head back and totally relaxed, when – splash! – Niña was in. She sat there – I swear, with a smile on her face – as if she always did this on a Saturday night. At least she had the tap end. Also, we have a huge American-style fridge with a water dispenser on the front: it is not plumbed in; rather it has a flask that takes five litres of bottled water. We are both big water drinkers, and it was usual for me to top up the flask every day. Suddenly we were using far more water than normal. One morning, I watched as Niña wandered into the kitchen, sniffed with disdain at the dogs' water bowl, went over to the fridge, stood up on her back legs and used a front paw to push the water-dispenser lever. Turning her head to one side, she greedily drank the chilled, bottled mountain-spring water that she had obviously acquired a taste for.

Nowadays, in summer she does two laps of the pool every morning before breakfast and then drinks from the hose pipe as we water the garden. Her front-left paw is at right angles to its leg; when we want to talk about her without her hearing her name, we call her 'my left foot'. We never have found out where she came from.

19

We Need a Project

Rodrigo, another of the large characters who seem to flourish in this tolerant land, is a Colombian jack of all trades, someone we met soon after moving here and thereafter bumped into pretty regularly. At one point he had a restaurant, at another an antiques business, and he always had a new plan. We would occasionally have a drink with him and enjoyed his company. A few years ago, his thing of the moment was a stall at the Sunday-morning *rastro*. The *rastro* is a mixture between a car-boot sale and an antiques market, where foreigners try to sell things I would be ashamed to put in the rubbish, and where the locals sell anything they deem to be old-fashioned but to us are often absolute treasures and bargains.

That particular morning, we had been to look at a little house for sale in the village. It was very charming but fully restored, and we were looking for a project, something for us to work on. There were two reasons for buying. First, when we had sold the UK business to fund our move, we had invested in the stock market; however, the expression 'too many eggs in one basket' often worried us. Spanish property prices were beginning to rise rapidly, and using Stephen's skills as an architect to restore an old house and then putting it on the holiday-rental market would keep our income in pace with inflation and hopefully give us capital growth: it made good financial sense. Second, it would give us a structure and purpose to our days and, best of all, an excuse to visit the antique shops, junk yards and obscure little craft workshops that we both enjoy so much.

When Rodrigo learned that we might possibly be in the 'property market', as he grandly called it, he insisted that we look at the house of his friend's wife in the next village.

This *was* a project. The terraced house is in the middle of Calle Real, the main street of the sleepy little village of Maro, no more than two miles east of Nerja, and had belonged to Rodrigo's friend's wife's mother. She had died many years earlier and the tiny house had been closed the following day: her daughter could not bear to enter – too many memories.

It was suspended in time. In the kitchen, a paper calendar, hanging by a nail from the flaking limestone wall, was showing July 1973. Even the bats that hung from the rafters didn't look that pleased with their squat. We began to climb the stairs, then someone shouted that it wasn't safe. From halfway up, we could see the single room ahead of us with a fireplace in the corner. The bed was still made up: sheets, pillows and a hand-stitched quilt. A water glass and a pair of wire-rimmed spectacles were on an old wooden chest by the bed and a pair of ladies' slippers neatly placed on the floor beside it. The roof had almost totally collapsed; much of it had landed on the bed. But, as usual, it was a beautiful day, and the sky looked azure through the gap. Outside the back door was a paved yard broken by jungle-sized weeds ending in a pile of stone that had once apparently been home to a mule. Rodrigo pointed out the worn path in the terracotta tiles from front door to back that was the result of many years of walking the mule in and out through the house every night and every morning. There was also a 'lean-to' – what can I call it without more information than you need or would want to know? – a toilet facility. I was wondering how Stephen was going to get us out of this politely.

'It needs a lot of work.'

Rodrigo and his friend shrugged.

'A new roof, of course, and a lick of paint.'

'More than that, how much are you asking?'

Why even ask? I was amazed. Polite is one thing, but *please*. We have learned over time that when talking to each other with Spanish friends around, many of whom speak at least some English, slang can be very useful. I opened my mouth to speak, but Stephen got there first.

'Button up.'

I buttoned. The price they mentioned was very, very low, but by this stage I would have almost paid that just to leave. I can only 'button' for so long and, knowing this, Stephen said he would 'think about it', and we left.

Maro has a great tapas bar, and we went there for lunch. Its reputation is built on its excellent seafood: we ordered mussels just plain steamed, so fresh it would be an insult to add anything; flash-fried *boquerones*, which are actually fresh anchovies, but nothing like the salty things that come with pizzas, more like baby sardines; *almejas*, tiny clams cooked in a garlic sauce; and *rosada*, the local white fish, pink hake, in a crisp, light batter. The rounds of fresh bread and garlic mayonnaise don't need ordering; they are assumed.

'What luck,' said Stephen.

'I think it's open every day, perhaps not Mondays.'

'Where?'

'Here.'

'No: what luck bumping into Rodrigo in the *rastro* and finding the house.'

'Very funny, but you got us out of it well.'

'I'm serious; it has great potential.'

'Oh dear. You are serious, aren't you?'

Years ago, when trying to explain an idea to a client, Stephen routinely reached into the left inside pocket of his suit jacket for a pen. This reflex has never gone, but the suits have, and his current uniform of polo shirts don't have pockets; so nowadays, that action kicks in my reflex to reach for my bag, where I always keep at least three pens and a scale rule.

Maro was the first, but not the last, of our houses to begin to be designed on a paper tablecloth. Basically what we were thinking of buying – and, indeed, did buy – was a space between two buildings. Nothing existed that could be saved or was actually worth saving apart from the fireplace in the kitchen and the front-door key, a good eight inches of rough iron. But it had potential, I was told.

Within days, the deal was done. I am sorry: if you want to read about the horror stories of buying a property in Spain, then this is not the book for you. The title deeds were in order, both lawyers and vendors turned up on time and, accepting the usual two-hour wait at the *notario*, it all went to plan. That evening we went to a local restaurant and, coincidentally, the friend of Rodrigo arrived with his wife and her aunts to celebrate the sale. After the meal, they invited us to their table for a drink and, as usual, I was expected to sit and talk to the women. During dinner we had been discussing a name for the house, and I asked María, the house's owner, what her mother's name had been. Carmen de la Valera. Casa del Carmen, we decided, would be a perfect name for the house and ensure that the name of one of the village's best-loved residents lived on.

Between buying the house and completing the final plaque ceremony, there were six months, a lot of work and a big learning curve. With the theory of 'better the devil you know' in mind, we asked Paco, our Frigiliana builder who had done many bits and pieces for us by this stage in both Casa Rosa and La Panificadora, if he would be interested in the work. He responded with what we have come to call the 'Frigiliana Shrug'.

Many years before, holidays in Casa Rosa with Stephen's young children often included taking Irene, Antonio's granddaughter, and Luisa, Mayte's daughter, with us on a trip to the beach. We found entertaining four is as easy as – even easier than – two. On one of these trips, after lunch at a beach restaurant, we asked them all if they would like an ice cream. We got three 'yes please's and a shrug of the shoulders from Irene, which we took to be a 'no'. So three ice creams were ordered and eaten. On leaving the beach a few hours later, again we offered ices.

'Annie. Ice cream?'

'Please.'

'Ben?'

'Yes.'

'Luisa. ¿Helado?'

'Sí. Gracias.'

'Irene –'

And before the question was out: 'Sí sí sí sí!'

She had, at the grand age of seven, learned very quickly that foreigners don't easily understand the Frigiliana Shrug.

Talking to Spanish friends, the Shrug is explained by the fact that this area had until 30 years ago been so very, very poor. Nowadays, to be seen not to need anything badly enough to show enthusiasm is a sign that you are not that badly off. This manner of exhibiting pride has been picked up by the children. We also see it in our everyday dealings with tradesmen: Stephen will stop someone in the street and almost beg for the bill for work completed five months before, and we get . . . the Shrug.

So Paco shrugged, and it was scheduled for his men to start work a few weeks later. He assured us that it would only be three months' work and that he could start in the middle of January. So we were quite relaxed when we signed a contract with our agents to have the house ready for rental by the end of June. Saturday the 28th was a date etched upon my brain.

Towards the end of February, we were getting seriously worried. Paco was not answering his phone. When our cars passed on the road, he would wave, smile and accelerate, ignoring our frantic gestures.

Lourdes and I had got into the habit since that very first day of having a cup of coffee together every morning before she began work. It helped my Spanish, and she brightened the day and was always full of the latest gossip from the village.

'You seem sad.'

'No, not sad, Lourdes: just a little worried about the house in Maro. Paco had promised to start work six weeks ago. We have to have it finished in June.'

'This is a problem for you? Yes?'

'If it is not finished, it will be a problem. Yes.'

This was an understatement. By this stage, I think we were both waking up in the middle of the night: Stephen vowing to find and kill Paco the next morning; me remembering the programmes on English television showing people who had booked their holidays and ended up on a building site. My worst nightmare featured a man named Cook standing with a microphone by our bedside.

Paco arrived that evening with the news that he would be starting work in Maro the following day. Nothing was ever actually said about the delay. Lourdes arrived the next day, observing that I appeared happier and that she was pleased to see it. Lourdes is an angel without the wings, and Paco, like most of the village people, is a relative. I once casually said to Lourdes that it seemed to me that she must be related to at least half of the people in the village. She was appalled.

'Jackie, please, please: far, far more than half.'

20

On Site

For Paco and his team of four, this project was a big step up. They were used to dealing with small building-works in and around the village, but had never rebuilt an entire house. Maro was at least a 20-minute drive away before the new road was built, which meant that it was not practical to go back to Frigiliana for meals. As always, they started at eight and stopped at ten for breakfast, a half-hour ritual during which they moved outside to sit either in the sun or the shade, depending on the temperature. The most junior of the labourers, Jorge, soon arrived back from the local bakery with freshly baked baguettes, which were cut open with a penknife. Huge overripe tomatoes would be squeezed onto the bread, followed by a tin of tuna or anchovies in olive oil. Jorge, Antonio Bigote, José and Sebastian washed these '*bocadillos*' (crusty bread rolls) down with a litre of water each and finished off with three or four oranges per person. Watching this every morning brought back vivid memories of a 'greasy spoon' two doors away from our office in London. There the windows were always running with steam, grease and condensation, and for breakfast or lunch, the clientele wanted double egg, bacon, fried slice, chips, beans and a tea with four sugars. Not many years ago in the UK, there was a revolutionary new discovery called the Mediterranean diet.

'Health and Safety' is not a term that goes hand in hand with Spain and building. Before anything could ever be built in Casa del Carmen, a lot had to be pulled down. The walls and ceilings were well over a hundred years old, and the original mud had turned to pure dust. The masks that Stephen bought were received with a polite nod and, like the hard hats, they then disappeared under a deep layer of exactly what they were supposed to protect the builders from. Jackhammers bounced noisily an inch or two away from the open-toed sandals worn by their operators, and when scaffolding was required, holes were knocked in the walls and planks pushed through and propped up on poles.

Work on the little house went well, but the weather was against us. April that year had many rainy days, and builders here not only don't work in the rain; they don't work at all on a day that begins with rain. We learned this early in the project: when waking up one morning to a downpour, we resigned ourselves to another lost day. But by ten the rain had stopped and the sun grew strong. We drove to Maro looking forward to seeing a hive of activity. Nothing. No one. Nada.

We went back to the village and spotted the car and motorbikes we recognised so well outside the favourite bar. Inside were our team. Their usual custom of meeting for a coffee and brandy at seven never changes; however, with the weather against them, this custom is prolonged and by ten in the morning, regardless of the improvement, it's too late and probably not advisable even to think about asking them to work that day.

By the beginning of June, we were really panicking. Paco seemed to think that the deadline of 28 June was when he had to finish his work, despite many conversations to the contrary. The reality was that when his guys finished, the whole house still needed a 'builders clean' before being painted with at least two coats over the bare concrete and, of course, being furnished. We tried to get them to finish one room at a time, but with a week to go, we still had them all over the house.

Once again, Lourdes came to the rescue. Despite Spanish machismo, women rule the houses here, and this was to be one of Lourdes's new houses. She arrived with *her* team: her two sisters and a cousin. No contest. The fiddly little jobs upstairs were finished that day. That, she instructed, left two days for them to finish downstairs before she would be working down there. They were like lambs to the slaughter. Yes, Lourdes; no, Lourdes; three bags full, Lourdes. It is the only time I have seen a big muscle-bound Spanish builder carrying a bucket of cement in each hand tiptoeing across the floor and looking behind him in fear of the dusty footprints he was leaving in his wake.

Friday, 27 June: we had ordered a hand-painted plaque from our favourite ceramics factory, owned by the professor of ceramics at Granada University, who is also responsible for replicating tiles in the Alhambra Palace, across the gorge from where he works. One of the final jobs for the builders when the house was rebuilt was to cement this plaque into the wall by the front door. To our surprise, most of the street arrived to witness the impromptu ceremony. Many of the older ladies who had grown up with Carmen had tears in their eyes. They pointed out the places in the house where, as young friends of Carmen, they had been allowed to stay overnight in the one bedroom shared by the whole family, all eight of them. Mathilda, the next-door neighbour, arrived, carrying two bunches of carnations. One bunch she gave to me, saying that she wished luck to us and all who stayed in the house. The other bunch, she explained, she would take to the church, where she would pray for God's blessing on the house and all who stayed there. Casa del Carmen de la Valera: a very grand name for a very small but very beautiful house. The last of the tiles were laid on the terrace; planters were planted with sweet-smelling jasmine, blue and white plumbago and gaudy geraniums; and we put the hosepipe into the empty pool mid-afternoon. Amazingly, it all came together. Inside, the bed was installed and made up, pictures were hung and bookshelves filled, and the kitchen was stocked with all that was needed to make a house a home.

Relieved, exhausted and very proud of what we had all achieved, we finished inside at about eight that evening, just as the builders finished outside. They didn't know that we had stocked the kitchen fridge full of beer until we pointed them in the right direction, and an impromptu party began. It was hot and the ten twelve-packs of San Miguel were disappearing faster than the pool was filling, but it didn't stop them. Bigote was first, diving from the steps into no more than three feet of water, and the rest were not far behind.

They left just before midnight. We cleaned up and then, without a word between us, we began a tour of the little house, spending four or five minutes in each room, remembering when and where we had bought this old door or that old chest, delighting in the end result of the walk-in shower built with more than two thousand tiny handmade tiles, and finally agreeing that using the traditional canes between the ceiling beams had been the right decision. We locked the door behind us at about two in the morning, and it felt like walking away from a new baby. If it was you who rented a house called Casa del Carmen in the village of Maro for two weeks from 28 June 1999, please breathe a big sigh of retrospective relief: you don't know how very close you were to sharing it with all of us.

21

People on Holiday

So, Casas Rosa and Carmen: two houses on the holiday-rental market. It was our habit to meet and greet our clients and show them around the houses. The agency did what was called a 'rep's visit'. This seemed to serve the purpose of confirming that holidaymakers had arrived at the right place, logging any complaints, selling guided tours and recommending restaurants – the 'don't forget to tell them Angela sent you and they'll look after you' sort of thing. Call me cynical, but it is amazing how often you could find Angela and friends eating in one of her 'must-try' but actually very average restaurants, though I never saw them pay a bill.

I can now look back and see how naive we were when we began to rent our houses. We had come from the 'customer-is-always-right' school. I still think it's a good school, but it seems that many customers have changed.

Nowadays, the compensation culture kicks in fast. Let me give you a small yet typical example: we bought some beautiful hand-crafted glasses in a village in the Alpujarras, six of each for wine, water and whisky. They were made of recycled glass with a blue tinge. We were equally proud of the dinner and side plates that we got from our man in Granada: a hand-painted set each with a different cheeky little bird in the centre. The letter of complaint had two points: one, the plates didn't match; and two, 'it is not possible to drink white wine from blue glass'. Only recently, in early 2009, we had a call to say that a lady staying in Casa Rosa last October had only just reported that she had left her jewellery box behind and was making an insurance claim for three thousand pounds! Wouldn't it be nice to have so much jewellery that it takes you five months to realise that the three thousand pounds' worth of the favourite pieces you took on holiday hadn't come back with you? It is the one and only time that we have had such an incident, but we decided a long time ago, after hearing horror stories from other owners of rented homes, that if it ever occurred, we would stand by 'our girls'. To use a local expression, they are 'as honest as Mary' and over the years have handed us two expensive watches, five pesetas, one hundred and thirty euros (more money than they make in a month with us), a wallet full of credit cards and a beautiful pair of diamond earrings – all of which we have sent, by registered post, back to their owners. (Not quite true: we kept the five pesetas.) We have never once received a note of acknowledgement, let alone a thank you.

I don't want to waste space here with stories of our beautiful things that have genuinely gone missing from our homes, or of the people who have left the houses almost in need of fumigation. (Actually I do – it would possibly be quite therapeutic – but I won't inflict it upon you.)

Anyway, most people are fine, and some are delightful. Soon after moving into La Panificadora, I met our Casa Rosa clients in the street. They were an elderly couple from Merseyside.

'Hello, how are you enjoying your holiday?'

'Right good.'

'Everything OK in the house?'

'Yup, haven't had a J-cloth out of me hand since I arrived; it's great.'

'The house was clean when you arrived, wasn't it?'

'You could have eaten off the floor, and that's the way I intend to keep it; it's right beautiful.'

True to her word, when they left we hardly knew they'd been.

Next came the mistress. I showed an elegant couple in their early fifties into the house one Saturday evening and invited them to join us for a drink the following lunchtime, as was our practice at the time. Stephen and Peter got on well immediately and walked through to the garden in animated conversation, leaving me sorting out drinks with Helen.

'White wine would be lovely.'

'And for your husband?'

I wasn't being formal; I just have a lousy memory for names and 'Peter' had evaded me for that moment.

'Peter's not my husband. He has a wife, of course, and two children. I'm the mistress, have been for over 25 years.'

This was actually more information than I wanted to know. It was not that I could possibly have grounds to be righteous about such things, just that I had a feeling that our habit of a quick drink with new arrivals was not going to turn out that way this time. Three hours later, we had the full story, whether we wanted it or not. They were both lawyers, and I found it vaguely amusing that she was a divorce specialist. Tuesday, Wednesday and Thursday nights they spent together at her flat (bought by him) in Kensington. Weekends she usually spent with friends, while he went 'home'.

'Christmases cost you a fortune, don't they, darling? He has to be with the family in Shropset, so he flies me to the sun, and, of course, I always have to have a little present from Peter to open, being all on my own on Christmas Day, don't I, darling?'

Last Christmas's 'little present' was flashed on a finger that could hardly support it.

Charly and Domingo helped, too; animals are a great ice-breaker. During the second year that we were renting out Casa Rosa, about ten of the couples or families from the year before returned to visit. We had exchanged Christmas cards with the parents, and their children had written to the cats and dogs. Most arrived armed with a stunning array of goodies from pet shops and even a pet superstore, a concept that the Spanish would have found impossible to understand. Lourdes begged me to put a packet of chocolate drops out of sight: chocolate was her weakness. She was open-mouthed when I pointed to the picture on the packet and explained that she wouldn't like them anyway; they were for the dogs. Toys sometimes arrived in the post, and Fernando, our postman, nearly jumped out of his skin when a parcel he was handing over squeaked loudly. Charly loved them all, but became particularly attached to anything torn, dirty or smelly. Domingo was more fussy: he went through a serious dinosaur phase, with a livid purple T. rex being his favourite.

It was actually the letters, emails and phone calls to family, friends and clients that became what you are reading now. Everyone was eager to know how we were all doing and enjoyed the stories. Had I been asked to sit down and write a book, it would never have happened.

22

José María

Yet another of the joys of living here is that we are able to spend much more time with José María. Many years ago, long before we had Casa Rosa, we spent a late June holiday in the little village of Montejaque, ten minutes north west of Ronda. We had rented what turned out to be a very basic self-catering cottage, the last house on the western edge of the village, and enjoyed many good, simple meals in the only one of the three village bars that served food. As usual in these places, mother was in the kitchen, father behind the bar and any children capable of not dropping plates helped out when necessary. In this case, the children were two boys of eighteen and fourteen. The eldest, José María, would serve our meals with style, taking care to lay the plastic table with its paper tablecloth and cheap cutlery as if he were handling fine linen and china; he would then linger in the hope of practising his minimal English. Within the first week, we had managed to establish that his aim was to work in England and learn the language, which would give him many more possibilities for a brighter future in Spain. He was saving and hoped to be able to afford to go there within three or four years.

At that time, Stephen was working on a big project designing SmithKline Beecham's new HQ below the Hammersmith flyover and, as it was nearing completion, recruiting temporary staff to supplement the furniture-installation crews. With a rush of blood to the head, which can happen to the best of us on holiday, we suggested on the last but one night that perhaps José María might like to come and work for us for three months starting that September, and live with us and learn the language. Obviously delighted by the offer, he would, of course, have to talk to his parents. The following night, they greeted us with open arms and tears.

We went home, we sent him his ticket and we found ourselves two months later standing in the arrivals hall at Gatwick Airport wondering what the hell we had done. We needn't have worried: Spanish waiters make the world's best long-term houseguests. José worked nights and we worked long days, and we would often come home to a Spanish tortilla cooked to his mother's recipe cooling in the kitchen. The secret is . . . drop the hot cooked, diced potatoes, onion and garlic into the cold, whisked raw eggs, stir, then leave them for at least 20 minutes before they hit the pan.

Everyone adored José María; they were naturally suspicious at first of someone hired by the managing director and staying in his house, but he was a very hard worker and as eager as a puppy to learn everything. The installation crews worked in pairs and from the start José was teamed with Ricky, one of the senior guys and an all-round good person, who adopted José. Ricky took him home to sample his wife's cooking and meet his kids, introduced him to his friends and his favourite pubs and clubs, and taught him to speak West Indian slang. Within a few days, on the rare occasions during the working week that we bumped into José at home, 'Hey man, what's going down?' was his usual greeting.

With José in tow at the weekends, we became tourists in London doing the usual touristy things: a trip down the Thames to Greenwich, visiting the Tower, the Palace and the art galleries. After three months, José's English was rather good. As we left for work early in the mornings, he would be arriving home and

winding down, usually in front of a video, and was especially fond
of a movie called *Uncle Buck*. By the time José left, he could recite
it word for word and we had found ourselves a friend for life.

The following May, we spent the Montejaque village fiesta
with him and his family; their bar was open twenty-four hours a
day for five days. María, his mother, proved that it is possible to
peel potatoes in your sleep, and as the last of the revellers were
thinking of going to bed at six or seven in the morning, the more
pious of the villagers were arriving for a coffee and *anís* before
the first Mass of the day. When we left at the end of a week,
José's father, Jacinto (I'm afraid the literal translation of Jacinto
is 'hyacinth'!), presented us with a set of keys to their house,
saying that now we would always have a home in Spain.

Two years later, we were back in Ronda to act as witnesses
at José's wedding to the beautiful Ana. The general informality
of Spanish life, their acceptance and tolerance of the needs of
every generation, continues around their ceremonies. The night
before the wedding, José, Ana, Stephen and I spent several hours
in the church, arranging the flowers and tying posies and cream
ribbons to the ends of each pew. The following day, we were the
first people to arrive in the church square, at about one thirty,
half an hour before the ceremony was due to start.

Had we not been there the night before, we would have
worried that we were in the wrong place: it was deserted. By
ten to two, however, people were beginning to appear. Everyone
stood outside chatting, but the huge old doors to the church were
still firmly shut. José, with his parents and brother, arrived on
foot on the dot of two and proceeded to mingle with the crowd,
greeting old friends, chatting and laughing. It was another 15
minutes before the car bearing Ana stopped in front of the
church, whose doors were *still* shut. José went to the car, helped
Ana out and took her hand, then together they walked up the
old stone steps, and José lifted the huge brass knocker and let
it drop. Immediately, a small Jew's Door opened and the priest

asked why they were here. My Spanish was just good enough to understand this, and I was in a complete panic: we had decorated the church the night before, family had arrived from all over Spain, a reception for 200 people was only hours away and the priest was asking why they were there.

'We wish to marry.'

'Then enter.'

It is a local tradition, and a rather charming one, if you are prepared for it. The doors were flung open, José and Ana walked down the aisle hand in hand, and they sat on the middle two of four chairs placed in front of the altar. José's mother and Ana's father sat on either side of them. I guess the fact that the stars of the show got seats should have given us a clue that this was not going to be quick. Parents of young children began emptying sacks of toys into the aisles, the kids settled down to play, and friends and relatives settled down to catch up on the year's gossip.

Nobody paid any attention to what was happening at the front for at least 40 minutes, until suddenly it seemed that José and Ana had been declared man and wife. At this point, everyone went around kissing everyone else, us included. They don't have 'his and hers' sides at a Spanish church wedding; in fact, quite the reverse: from the moment you walk into the church behind the couple, they see it as two families and groups of friends merging. For the rest of the day, and well into the following morning, the party continued, and now, years later, I jump every time the phone rings, hoping it is the call to say that we are godparents once again.

While in Ronda, José suggested that we go to the corrida, the bullfight. Ronda is home to the oldest bullring in the country, built in the early eighteenth century. José proudly told us that it is the dream of every aspiring matador to appear there. Bullfighting is second only to football in Spain as a spectator sport, and yet in the newspapers here, it is usually reported in the arts section rather than the sports pages.

Of course, me being me, I shouldn't even have considered it. I knew I wouldn't like it, but stubbornly I wanted to be able to say that I had formed that opinion from experience, not hearsay. I know, I know, I know. We queued for our tickets and, given the option of *sol o sombre* – sun or shade – chose the more expensive shade. It was to begin at five on an early September afternoon. It started well: the three matadors, each to face two bulls, paraded around the ring in their stunning *traje de luces* (suit of lights), beautiful hand-beaded trousers, great bums and cropped jackets that literally sparkled in the early evening sunshine. They were accompanied by their team of *banderilleros* and *picadores*. Although I didn't realise it at the time, these are the ones who, on foot and on horseback, stick spears into the poor little things (OK, I know they are huge, but they are defenceless) before the matador finally finishes them off. If the matador achieves a clean kill, he is awarded one of his victim's ears. If he has been especially brave, he also gets the tail. Whoopeee! It was balletic. The men's bravery and skill was breathtaking, but the bottom line is that the minute those bulls enter the ring, they don't stand a chance: even if they get lucky and kill the matador, they will still be killed anyway. I left after the first bull, arranging to meet Stephen outside later, having achieved what I had set out for: the ability to say from experience that bullfighting is most definitely not for me.

I found a cafe opposite the bullring, ordered a strong coffee and indulged in one of my own favourite sports: people-watching. Two large refrigerated trucks pulled up at the back entrance of the arena, and a group of men jumped down from the high cabs. They threw white coats over their day clothes and pulled on wellington boots. The penny didn't drop. It wasn't until they began to unpack very professional-looking cleavers and knives that I realised they were the butchers preparing to . . . Yes.

That evening Stephen ate steak; I ordered a salad. Bullfighting and bull-eating are most definitely not for me.

23

So Here We Are

So there we were: the years had flown by, we had three dogs, three cats and three houses. Still not a Spanish pointer or Mediterranean tabby, but the village had adopted us and it certainly felt like home. English people living here would sometimes ask 'do you go home often?' and didn't seem to understand our response that we went home every day. I was invited to nativity plays, swimming galas and children's birthday parties, and Stephen went into the mountains on shooting parties, although he didn't carry a gun.

In early January, the thrushes fly down from the mountain pines to eat the olives, and the hunters wait until twilight, at about six in the evening, and shoot the ready-stuffed birds on their return. In the early '40s, at the end of the civil war, Gerald Brennan writes in *South from Granada* of the eerie stillness of a land without birds. Then people were starving; the birds were all killed and eaten. Today it is more for sport, although the waste-not-want-not culture remains, and the few they shoot are taken home, plucked and cooked. It seems like a lot of effort for little reward: a plucked thrush makes a poussin look obese. Around this time Stephen also renewed his love of football, becoming a season-ticket holder and passionate supporter of Málaga football club. Social activities here are still segregated.

We had permanent suntans. Stephen was a dark mahogany and I was forever nagging him about wearing a cap and using a factor-30 cream. I was more of a light beige and much more careful. It is yet another sad fact of ageing that older men look better with a good tan, while most women look as if they need ironing.

His other new passion was the disease that can render the most innocent and educated of people capable of almost nothing else. It affects conversation, lifestyle and dress code. It goes by the innocent name of 'golf'.

'I had an eight on the fifth today.'

'Well done, darling.'

'You're not listening.'

'Yes I am. An eight on the fifth, very impressive.'

'It's a par three.'

'Very, very well done.'

I do try to show enthusiasm – honestly I do – it's just that the game seems so futile. One week Stephen has triumphed at the ninth, and the following week it is that same ninth that has ruined not only his whole score, but his life, too. Meanwhile, I have been indulging my love of gardening and have little things growing as a reward for my efforts. His rewards are often huge ugly cups that sit on the top shelf of our airing cupboard until they are won the following year, again destined for the next airing cupboard – or so I suspect. Occasionally, he will return triumphant with a voucher for a meal for two (excluding wine and to be used on a Tuesday or Thursday) at a restaurant that we would pay not to go to. What finally finished it for me was overhearing a very loud woman wearing head-to-toe Burberry golf clothes and braying to a friend.

'Well, darling, as I always say: if you can't play . . . *dis-play*.'

24

Just an Idea

In our third year here, I began spending one morning a week helping out at the Taller de la Amistad, a workshop for mentally-handicapped young people. It had been started five years earlier by an amazing lady whose own son is handicapped, though compared with many of her subsequent charges, only mildly so. Here, when a child is born with any form of impairment, the family close ranks and every member is expected to pull their weight in the added burden of keeping a child more or less behind closed doors. From listening to Gloria, the lady who started the workshop, these children are usually very well treated — often, they are thoroughly spoiled — but just not allowed to be part of what we call 'normal' society.

Her vision was to integrate these youngsters into the local community. By providing the resources to create a workshop, they could, with encouragement and help, produce saleable items, thereby becoming more valued members of their community. Here, what you contribute within your capability, not what you do or what you earn, is still of the greatest importance. Gloria worked tirelessly, and still does, not only with the youngsters, but also at creating fundraising events for the whole scheme. She badgers the town hall and local businesses for support and sponsorship, and charms all the local performers into giving their acts for free.

It was at a Christmas fundraising dinner for the workshop in the smartest hotel on the coast that Stephen did it again: he came up with a seemingly casual thought that was to change our lives for the next few months.

We had taken a table for ten and, knowing that there was to be flamenco dancing and *sevillana* singing as part of the after-dinner entertainment, we invited Lourdes, Charo and their husbands to join us. (Charo, Lourdes's elder sister's sister-in-law, began working with us when we needed a cleaner for Casa del Carmen, and I still enjoy the Saturday cleaning rota that starts 'Charo in Maro and Rosa in Rosa'.)

Watching the show, which was good, I was more entertained by Lourdes than by the acts themselves. She was both mesmerised and animated. Her top half was rigid, chin propped up by hands, elbows on the table and mouth open. Like a swan, all the work was going on below the surface: beneath the tablecloth, her feet, squashed into strappy, outrageously high heels, were tapping and twisting.

'Just look at Lourdes: she's loving it.'

'We thought she would.'

'Just imagine if she lived in London. If this is her reaction to this, can you imagine what she would be like seeing a West End show?'

'Take her.'

'What?'

'Take her.'

'To London?'

'Yes.'

'Take Lourdes to London, to see a show?'

'Yes. It's just an idea, but you haven't been back for almost three years. Do some shopping, visit friends and take Lourdes with you for company and to see a West End show. It would be fun.'

'Are you having an affair?'

'Yes. With a very attractive goat. So go to London for a few days, leave me in peace, go and have some fun.'

The coffees and brandies arrived at our table. I wasn't sure how or even when to suggest that Lourdes might like to come to London with me, but something told me that it was a suggestion better made in public, and here we were. If she went home and days later told Julio of the offer, then I felt that the whole thing would literally never get off the ground.

'Lourdes, you enjoyed the show?'

'It was the best I have ever seen. The dancers were fabulous, the singer had such a great voice, true? No? And the guitarist, he is my younger sister's husband's cousin. I had heard that he was very good, but I have never seen him play before.'

'In London there are many theatres with shows, certainly as good, possibly even better than this, performing every night.'

'Every night?'

'Yes. At least 20 different shows, all within an area the size of the village. Stephen has an idea. He has suggested that you and I should go to London for a couple of days and see a show. He will pay for it as a birthday present for me. What do you think?'

Charo started clapping and laughing, 'Go, Lourdes, go.'

Lourdes laughed, smiled and looked at Julio. His face was unreadable. She turned to us again.

'Me. I go to London. London, England. I have never spent one night away from the village. It is not possible. It is beyond my dreams.'

'OK, forget it. It was just an idea.'

Again, she looked at Julio. He is a man of few words. He leaned forwards slowly and placed his not inconsiderable forearms on the table. We all held our breath.

'Thank you. Thank you very much; it is a most kind offer. Lourdes would love to go to London.'

Everyone at the table cheered.

Una Pregunta – A Question

We booked the flights for late May. By the end of January, the whole village knew that Lourdes was going to London. Every time she arrived at La Panificadora, she had a new question.

'Jackie. *Una pregunta.*'

'Yes, Lourdes?'

'Will I need a passport? Someone said that I would.'

Stupidly, I was only just beginning to realise what a really big deal this was going to be for her. Of course she needed a passport, and of course, never having spent a night outside of Frigiliana, she had never needed one before.

'Stephen. *Una pregunta.*'

'Yes, Lourdes?'

'My father says that it is dangerous to fly and that we would be much safer driving to London, and that it would be quicker, too.'

'Don't worry, Lourdes: it will be much quicker and much safer to fly, especially with Jackie's driving. Trust me.'

'*Una pregunta*: my father says that when we fly, we will be nearly as high as the clouds.'

'Lourdes, when you fly you will be much higher than the clouds, you will be able to look down on them.'

Crossing herself, she made Stephen promise that he wouldn't repeat this to her father or she would never be allowed to go.

The questions continued for four months: what should she pack, how much money did she need, would she be able to speak to her family while she was away, should she bring her own food. Excitable at the best of times, the tensions were rising and she was totally impossible in the final week before we left.

26

Lourdes Goes to London

On that sunny Tuesday morning in late May when we collected Lourdes from the village, all of her family and many of her friends had turned up to wave her off. She, her mother, grandmother and both her sisters were all crying and clinging to each other. I began to think we had made a mistake. She had borrowed a suitcase from us at least two months before, saying that she wanted to start packing early and be sure that she didn't forget anything. Judging by the weight of it, she certainly hadn't.

Sitting in the back of the car on the way to the airport, she was uncharacteristically quiet, not surprising, though, considering the trip to Málaga was a huge event in itself. Then, after about half an hour:

'Jackie, did you find it difficult to have to cook 11 different meals all at once?'

'Eleven meals? What do you mean, Lourdes?'

'Lunch and supper for today, and we won't be back until late on Friday, so I cooked 11 meals. Carmina is going to serve the suppers, and my mother and Aurora are doing the breakfasts and lunches between them.'

'Shut up, Lourdes.'

I had felt until then that I had more than fulfilled my housewifely duty by leaving a casserole in the fridge for that night, and ample sandwich fillings, after which Stephen was on his own.

Málaga now has a sizeable airport with an impressive new departures hall, the first of many things that over the next few days were going to take Lourdes's breath away. She cried again when Stephen left us in the queue to check in.

'Lourdes, this is supposed to be a happy time, it's an adventure.'

'I have never been so happy in my life.'

More crying.

Normally I would say that the flight was uneventful. It was, but then I was seeing it through the eyes of a pretty seasoned traveller. This time, though, it was a joy to see it through new eyes, those of a first-time traveller, and that was indeed the beauty of the whole three days that Lourdes and I spent in London.

We were flying with Iberia, the Spanish national airline, which both eased and complicated things, as all signs and instructions were always first, and often only, in Spanish.

'Jackie, why do we need life jackets?'

'Jackie, why do we need oxygen masks?'

'Jackie, what are life jackets and oxygen masks?'

Usually a calm passenger, I was beginning to ask myself the same questions.

I think Lourdes was the only person on that plane who was glued to the safety briefing as we taxied to the runway, to the point of undoing her seatbelt – not an easy feat – and getting up to look behind her at the rear exits as they were pointed out. The usual short-haul economy-airline lunch became a feast of discovery. She sat in the window seat and squeaked and squawked all the way to London.

Heathrow. As if travelling with a child, I was in charge of tickets and passports, and it was here that I had begun to realise the extent to which Spanish *camposinos* have a respect, yet mistrust and fear, of officialdom.

'My passport is new. Will that be a problem?'

'No, don't worry.'

'I have never had one before. Will that be a problem?'

'No problem.'

'My picture is not very good. Julio says it looks more like my mother. Will that be a problem?'

We sailed through customs and picked up our bags.

'We stand still here and our bags will find us?'

Luckily they did, and I pushed the always defiant baggage trolley towards the taxi rank. This involved meeting Lourdes's next new experience, the revolving door. Heathrow's revolving doors are huge, designed to get as many people as possible, together with said trolleys, through quickly. In the middle of these contraptions are glass windows displaying the latest, no longer duty free, perfume and jewellery promotions. Lourdes was mesmerised. Concentrating on steering the trolley, it was a few minutes before I realised that she had done at least six circuits. On her next lap, I reached in and fished her out.

The driver of the black cab that took us into central London was as friendly and chatty as I fondly remembered most London cabbies to be.

'What lingo's that then?'

'Sorry?'

'Language, love, what are you two speaking?'

'Oh, Spanish.'

'Thought I recognised it, I've been to Malta on holiday.'

Surprise, surprise, it was raining. The new fast lane on the M4 was a wonderful regulation as I was in a taxi. Though I am sure that had I still been in the company car and therefore destined for the other two lanes, I would have been cursing like hell. As it was, we sailed into town.

'Julio would love it here: it's so green, his goats would be so very happy.'

Lourdes had borrowed a camera from a friend, a simple point-and-snap camera that would feature frequently on this trip. Seven hours in, we already had photos of us leaving the village, photos of Málaga Airport, the plane through the window of the departure lounge and of the baggage hall at Heathrow. Now Lourdes would not let the taxi driver go until he had posed with her while I snapped. He was charming and seemed almost flattered by the request; maybe he had done the same in Malta.

It was early evening, about seven thirty. We checked into the hotel and, leaving Lourdes in her room with instructions on how to lock the door, not to open it to anyone and to call me if she had any problems, I promised to be back in an hour. That evening we were going to meet John, a good friend of ours whom Lourdes had met several times in Spain. John and I had agreed the week before that we would meet outside the Odeon in Leicester Square and go for a meal in Chinatown.

Knock knock. 'Lourdes, it's me.'

'How do I know?'

'How do you know what?'

'That it's you? You told me not to open the door to anyone.'

'Yes, but this is *me*, Lourdes, *me* who told you not to open the door, so open the door, OK, please just open the door.'

Inside the room, it quickly became clear why her suitcase had been so heavy. In the space of that hour, she had turned her room into a shrine. There were three statues of Jesus, four of local saints (including Sebastian and Antonio), many crosses, two sets of rosary beads (good Catholics always carry a spare) and pictures of all her family.

When John and I had spoken, 'in front of the Odeon in Leicester Square' had seemed like a very easy and traditional place to arrange to meet. What neither of us had known at the time was that it was the opening night, the London premiere, of the latest Bond movie. Traffic was backed down Piccadilly and we got out of the taxi halfway, paying and apologising to the cabbie, who grunted and did a swift U-turn.

London instincts, in hibernation for three years, quickly kicked in. Knowing that we were very late, I grabbed Lourdes's hand and pulled and pushed us through the crowds. There were more lights, traffic and people in and around Piccadilly Circus than at any Andalucían village gathering, and here, all of them were strangers. Lourdes was like a rabbit caught in headlights; she was terrified.

Chinatown, possibly, was not the best choice for our first meal in London. The idea had been to expose her to as many new experiences as possible in only three days. That was arranged before we left, before I had even begun to understand that most of the things I took for granted were going to be new experiences for her anyway. The first night away from her village and her family, her first plane journey, a new country – she had never left Andalucía, let alone Spain – not speaking the language, the scale of London, the height of its buildings . . . The list was already almost endless, and we had only been gone for ten hours.

She was brilliant. She greeted John with such enthusiasm, a familiar face, very welcome at that stage, and then sat with her mouth open as the usual range of Chinese food arrived.

Crispy duck with pancakes rolled and eaten with fingers were a big hit, and the chopsticks caused hilarity. Her approach was to take one in each hand and use them as spears. It was successful with the deep-fried prawns, but failed miserably with the seaweed. The laughter coming from our table drew the waitresses, who were enchanted. I still can't quite put my finger on it, but there are now so many times when I have watched Lourdes work her innocent magic. People love her. The Chinese girls gave her chopstick lessons. After a memorable meal, we paid the bill and decided to walk down to Trafalgar Square: it would be easier to find a taxi there, and the lion statues, fountains and Nelson would be Lourdes's last sightseeing hit and photo opportunity of the night. We were both tired.

'Please, please wait. For you.'

Our waitress was running after us down the street with a pair of chopsticks and a pretty little blue-and-white china bowl. She smiled, bowed and gently presented them to Lourdes, who kissed her heartily on both cheeks. It all seemed so natural, good and kind: words that I had stopped associating with London in my last few years living there.

27

OK: Let's Shop

Eight thirty next morning: very late for Lourdes and rather early for me, we sat in the breakfast room. I was translating the quite extensive menu, and she was trying to get her brain around the fact that you sat down to a breakfast that was delivered to the table (although her husband and son had mastered that one years ago).

'*Dos zumos de naranja, dos cafés con leche, y tostadas para dos tambien, por favor.*'

'*Vale, ¿algo mas?*'

'*Nada, gracias.*'

It took several seconds after the young girl had walked away for my early morning brain to register that we were in a London hotel, that I had just ordered our breakfast in Spanish and that, hopefully, I had been understood. She returned with our juices and we established that she was a language student from Galicia working breakfast shifts at the hotel. For Lourdes, it was reassuring, comforting, almost a bit of home.

We walked in the rain through the north of Hyde Park towards Marble Arch. Shopping in England after a three-year absence, it seemed to make sense to hit Marks & Spencer first for the basics, after which we could have some fun. It was still early, and there were what I had sadly become so used to many years before: people sleeping in doorways. I saw them out of the corner of my eye, but then resurrected my London tunnel vision and continued walking. Lourdes stopped.

'Jackie. There is a young man asleep here.'

'Yes, Lourdes. Come on, let's go.'

'But why is he asleep here?'

'Probably because he has nowhere else to go.'

'But London is rich. It is a rich city.'

'Yes. That is why poorer people come here.'

'Without their family? Where are his family? Why don't they look after him?'

I have always enjoyed M&S's Marble Arch store. I know they have had a bad press, but for me their bog-standard stuff is fine and just occasionally they come up trumps (as you can tell, I'm never going to be a fashion writer). For Lourdes, who loves to shop in the village's one and only clothes shop or at the clothes stall at the weekly street market, this was all her birthdays and Christmases arriving at once. When I was a busy working woman, the food hall was a godsend for mid-week supper parties with tarted-up versions of their food. Add a few fresh mushrooms and a bit of parsley, and casually pretend that you threw it together yourself in the copious spare time you manage to organise between doing deals, learning a new language and, of course, going to the gym. Don't try and tell me that you haven't cheated too. It was also useful to be able to buy clothes in a lunch hour, try them on at leisure at home and, if necessary, return them without hassle. In fact, I don't think I had ever seen the inside of their changing rooms. This was about to change.

Almost two hours later, having tried on their whole spring collection in every colour, Lourdes bought a skirt. We moved on to accessories. Lourdes loves hats and, coming up to wedding season, the place was full of them. She was particularly taken with a huge pink-straw top hat, similar in shape and size to that worn by the Mad Hatter in *Alice in Wonderland*.

'Lourdes, you look wonderful, I must have a photo.'

She posed, hands on hips and at the last minute stuck her tongue out. Click. We were both giggling like teenagers. I popped the camera back in my bag and had begun to move on when there was a hard tap on my shoulder. Behind me was a dragon with flaring nostrils dressed in an M&S uniform with a badge saying supervisor – no name, just supervisor – pinned to her impressively large chest.

'I've called security.'

'Excuse me?'

'It is forbidden to take photographs within the store. There is a sign.'

'Oh, sorry, I must have missed it.'

'Well, you will be watched, and if you try to take any more photographs, we will be forced to ask you to leave.'

I was two seconds away from letting rip, but then saw the look on Lourdes's face: total confusion and worry; she didn't understand a word, but she certainly understood the tone.

We turned and left the shop.

'Why was she angry, what did I do wrong?'

'Nothing. You, *we*, did absolutely nothing wrong, forget it, don't worry.'

A minute later we were in Selfridges, and it didn't take her long to forget. Lourdes's first escalator took a bit of getting used to. Stupidly, seeing that she was apprehensive, I stepped on to show her how it was done, by which time I was committed. Seeing me disappearing before her eyes, she took a big breath and jumped with both feet. We worked from the top down: every good shopper has a plan. The designer-clothes floor had prices that left Lourdes awestruck, with snooty assistants to match. The toy department offered electric cars for children that were worth more than most of the old Seats in the village, and stuffed toys bigger than any of her husband's goats. Finally, the ground-floor perfumery. It had not changed, still an assault course of pretty, overly made-up young and not-so-young things trying to spray you as you passed.

Instead of the purposeful stride and tight, polite shake of the head that I had perfected over the years, Lourdes stopped as soon as anyone approached her. She smiled and pushed her wrist out to try perfumes, the back of her hand for lipsticks or eye-shadow colours. She eagerly climbed onto a little stool in full view of everyone to have her eyelashes curled, and happily allowed her chipped nail varnish to be removed from two nails and repainted so that the girl from Estée Lauder could let her 'experience' a new shade. We were in there for over an hour. Obviously she didn't understand a word that was being preached about the lifting benefits of this or the tightening results of that; in fact, she didn't buy a single thing, yet we walked out with enough free samples to keep her and her sisters in cosmetics for a year. How does she do it?

A brief moment of total panic: I'd lost her. I'd left the shop through swing doors while Lourdes chose to resume her affair with the revolving ones. Only two circuits this time – she was learning fast – but what if I had actually lost her? She wouldn't even know the name of our hotel. We went for a coffee, and I began to talk to her as I would talk to a small child.

'Lourdes, we must make a plan for what to do if we lose sight of each other. London is much bigger and busier than Frigiliana.' A look of panic swept over her face. I went on quickly. 'It won't happen, of course, but better to be safe. Yes? Good. If you can't find me, stand still, don't move and I will find you. Take this card: it has the name and address of our hotel. If I haven't found you after half an hour, give it to a taxi driver: they are all along here, look, big black cars with yellow lights at the front. The driver will take you back to the hotel, and I will come and find you. OK?' I resisted the strong temptation to tie a baggage label to her in Paddington Bear fashion.

On we went: Debenhams, John Lewis, BHS and every little shop between the major stores up to Oxford Circus. A right turn into Regent Street: Liberty, Burberry, Aquascutum, but only serious window-shopping at Mappin & Webb.

For lunch, we met up with a gaggle of my girlfriends, three of whom had already met Lourdes in Spain, and she greeted them like long-lost friends. In fact, I was almost jealous. (Not true: I was really, really jealous.) They made much more of a fuss of her than of me, and they all had little presents for her. As we tucked into our genuine Italian pizzas cooked in a genuine Italian pizza oven, it occurred to me that the three meals we had eaten since arriving – Chinese, continental breakfast and now the pizza – were, in fact, typical English food.

The afternoon, what was left of it, we spent in the new Waterstone's in Piccadilly, armed with a list of at least 20 'must-buy' books for Stephen. It was the days before we had discovered the joys of Amazon, and a lack of English-language bookshops in our part of Spain was one of the few things we could find to moan about.

New experience number 406: the London Underground. Earlier when we had walked past a tube station, I had tried to explain the concept to Lourdes, but I don't think that she actually believed me. We descended into the dirty, smelly, hostile environment that I had forgotten existed. It was almost five, and the rush hours were beginning. A busker was sitting cross-legged in one of the spaces at the bottom of the escalator, which Lourdes had this time tackled with mounting confidence, though still using the two-feet-first-and-jump approach. Always enchanted by any music, she stopped dead in her tracks at the bottom. This time I was behind her – I was learning, too. The resultant pile-up and muttered curses sailed over her head (there are advantages to not being able to speak the language). She could not be moved on, so I manoeuvred her into a corner and let her enjoy the music. When the song was finished, she rushed over, stood in front of the bemused young man so obviously used to being ignored, and clapped loudly. With a final '*olé*', she returned to me without having put any money in his guitar case, but when I glanced guiltily behind as we walked on, he was sitting there grinning after us.

Westbound on the Central Line, always shoulder to shoulder, and often face to face, but never eye to eye with total strangers. For someone with an English vocabulary of 30 words maximum, Lourdes sure knew how to use them, albeit in total innocence.

'Hello.'

The business-suited man hanging by one hand from the overhead rail, reading a quartered *Evening Standard*, recoiled and turned away. Until she had uttered that simple word, she had been fated to stand with her nose in his armpit, although probably not a problem for someone accustomed to 300 goats. The woman on her other side got the same greeting. Lourdes got the same response. She looked at me, shrugged and smiled, not having a clue that on her first tube journey, without any pointy elbows or aggression, she had managed to achieve what the regular commuters had been after for years – a bit of space.

That evening, Wednesday, was to be dinner with Julia, our old Spanish teacher (or, rather, our Spanish teacher of old). It served the dual purpose of meeting up with a good friend while giving Lourdes a chance to speak in her own language. When planning this short trip, it became difficult to find the time to see everyone that I would have liked without intruding on the most important aspect of all: letting Lourdes see London. So I combined two reunions, with friends who had never met. Weeks before, Julia had insisted that we must come to dinner and see her new flat. Clive, a long-term friend and colleague, had made the same offer, having just moved to Twickenham. Knowing who was by far the best cook, I accepted Julia's offer and asked if Clive could come too.

There was also a subplot here. Julia was at the time going through a 'what is the meaning of life thingy' and had left her boyfriend of 12 years. Clive had just been dumped by the latest love of his life. Stephen could see what I had in mind.

'It won't work.'

'What won't work?'

'Clive and Julia. Not in a million years.'

'Don't know what you're talking about. It's just dinner.'

'I know you and your scheming, and I'm telling you it won't work.'

It worked in a way. In fact, the mere thought of a relationship with Clive – probably one of London's most eligible bachelors, but just not her type – speeded up her return to Moyses, so clouds and silver linings anyway. Regardless of the very obvious lack of potential romance, it was still a lovely evening. We got back to the hotel in one piece, despite a scream from Lourdes that made the taxi driver swerve dramatically. She saw a train, her first train, ever, so she screamed, very loudly. Seemed reasonable to me.

28

Day-trippers

Breakfast. Day two. The same waitress.

'Hello, Lourdes, how are you? Enjoying London? Would you like the same as yesterday, and what about your friend?'

Lourdes asked me if I wanted the same as yesterday, a question that I had fully understood. How the tables had turned within 24 hours.

'Please, yes, we will both have the same. How was college yesterday?'

They chatted for at least five minutes: the girl from Galicia and the 'girl' from Andalucía in a London hotel.

The previous morning, walking to the shops, we had been accosted in the most charming way by several guides for the many open-top double-decker tour buses that trawl the city. This had never happened to me in the 20 years I had lived in London. How, then, after only four years in Spain had I come to look like a tourist? Or was it Lourdes?

We joined the bus at the Bayswater stop, nearest to the hotel, having bought 'hopper' tickets that allowed us to jump on and off any bus at any point throughout the day. First in the queue, we raced up the stairs and sat at the front, plugging in the headphones and selecting the right languages, or at least trying to. Understanding that we could get off, go to see things, then catch the next bus, Lourdes at first wanted to get off at every stop. I pointed out that our plane left at two the next day and therefore this would not be possible. We became more selective. We 'hopped' at the Houses of Parliament: she was enchanted by Big Ben; she had seen it on news reports on Spanish television, but couldn't believe how big it was. At twenty to eleven, I bought outrageously overpriced, weak coffee from a stall on Westminster Bridge and we sat at Churchill's feet in Parliament Square waiting for the chimes. To this day, whenever our newspaper has a picture of Big Ben, we save it for her; she has started a scrapbook. More hopping for the Tower of London and St Paul's, and then Harrods and Harvey Nicks for additional retail therapy. Finally we left the tour at Buckingham Palace, by which time Lourdes knew far more about the history of London than I did. In all of the six buses that we had used, not one had an English soundtrack that worked. Lourdes's statements, such as 'interesting about the little boy in the Great Fire' or 'fancy that happening in the Tower', were totally lost on me.

Lunch was a sandwich at a Pret A Manger. I bought Brie and tomato, and Lourdes announced that she loved English cheese! I quickly decided that bringing France into the frame at this stage would be more information than was necessary. Sitting on stools in the window, I was thoroughly enjoying the view of London life through her new eyes.

'People walk and eat.'

'Of course.'

'But they walk and eat all at the same time, and talk, too, with a phone in their other hand, and they don't look at each other, or say hello, it is as if the people around them do not exist.'

And:

'When is siesta?'

'There isn't one.'

'No siesta? No sleep of the keys?'

This is a very old-fashioned expression, based on the traditional siesta when, after lunch, the man of the house would, still sitting at the table, rest his head in his arms with the big old door key, much like the one we inherited when we bought Casa del Carmen, clenched in his fist. When the key dropped and woke him, it was time to go back to the fields.

Next was Covent Garden to see the street performers and shop in the covered market. This was a great hit. Market-shopping was something Lourdes understood, and she picked up several little gifts for her family. Lourdes loves any form of entertainment, and there was a particularly good selection in the piazza that day. A limbo dancer, a fire-eater that drew squeaks of excitement from her, a girl with a pet monkey dressed in Victorian costume offering to let you pose with it for photos, at a price, of course. Lourdes was so enchanted by the little creature that against my principles, I paid and snapped. To this day, it is one of her favourite photos of the trip. The definite favourite, though, was the human statue. At first she would not believe it was a real man painted top to toe in silver. He was very good: so good, in fact, that I was almost beginning to wonder myself, when suddenly he reached for his three-cornered hat, doffed it with a flourish and immediately resumed his pose. Lourdes had to have a closer look. She marched up to him and stood on tiptoe with her face no more than a foot from his and her fists tucked into her hips. For a good minute he didn't flinch, then he winked at her, she screamed, the crowd laughed and Lourdes ran and hid behind me. We sat in the weak but welcome sunshine, me with a glass of wine and she, as always, with water, and we watched the world go by.

'So many people. There are more people here, in this square now, than live in my pueblo. No one will ever believe all that I have seen.'

'Yes they will, and anyway, we will have the photos to prove it.'

Drinks at six with yet more people familiar to Lourdes. In fact, it was no more than three weeks since Paul and Judy had been staying with us. Judy, as always, immaculate in Armani, was already at the Opera House bar when we arrived, and Paul appeared soon after. She has a crisis-management company and is her own best PR; she always seems totally unflappable. If oil spilled from any of my tankers (her speciality), I would call Judy. The champagne was on ice, and with a nod of her beautifully coiffed head, a plate of giant prawns was delivered to the table. Prawns were the perfect choice, of course, something that didn't faze Lourdes at all; she rolled up her sleeves, revealing beefy, tanned arms, and peeled twenty to our two. We had just over an hour together before it was time to make for the theatre. Goodbyes, like hellos, are not things to be rushed in Spanish. Lourdes bestowed blessings on both of them, their families, their health and their wishes for the future. She promised that she would go to church next week to ask for their swift return to Spain. I thought calling easyJet would probably have better results, but kept that to myself and just translated.

29

The Show

'Take Lourdes to see a West End show' was how the idea for this trip had begun. When the seeds of the idea became saplings, Which Show? became a serious point of discussion. Predictably, Stephen, with his logical mind, after a 24-hour gap, came up with the answer.

'Cats.'

'What have they done now? If it's the new flowerbed again, I swear I'll kill them.'

'Cats. It's obvious.'

'I can't see them. Where?'

'*Cats*. The musical. Lourdes won't be able to understand a play; you need to take her to see something that doesn't need words, and she loves animals. Book for *Cats*.'

The theatre had been home to the show for many years. Once you saw the stage set, you realised it was no surprise that it rarely travelled. The foyer, however, was the typical red-plush affair. I bought the programme, the T-shirt, and ordered our drinks, wine and water, for the interval. The bell rang and we entered the auditorium.

The story, obviously about cats, is set in a rubbish dump with the audience in the middle of it. To get to our seats, we had to navigate five-foot-long sardine cans and cornflakes packets. On stage, there was the rusty bonnet of an old car wreck, a sofa with its stuffing spewing out and a pile of builders' rubble that made me feel quite at home.

Lourdes was very quiet. We sat in row three, Lourdes in the aisle, with me to her right.

'What do you think, Lourdes?'

'Jackie, Charo and I would do very well here. I think they need a cleaner.'

I opened my mouth to respond, but was saved in the nick of time as the theatre lights dimmed.

It was a magical performance. From the opening song, we were both enchanted. The 'cats' were dressed in skintight leotards painted to look like real markings; we had ginger toms, black-and-white moggies, Mediterranean tabbies and even a Siamese. They arrived onstage from all over the theatre, crawling on all fours up the aisles, even abseiling down from the balconies, stopping en route to brush up against members of the audience. Across the aisle from Lourdes was a city type with whom I assume were his wife and children. A cat started to rub itself against his leg; he sat there, staring straight ahead, obviously rigid with embarrassment, poor man. The next cat to enter through our aisle targeted Lourdes, who was delighted. She stroked its head and rubbed under its chin, all the while exclaiming loudly, '*Mi gato, mi gato, Jackie, miras mi gato tan bonito.*' ('My cat, my cat, Jackie, look at my beautiful cat.')

Next came a beautiful tortoiseshell that headed straight for us. Lourdes went through the same performance and then, in heavily accented English, came out with one of her few English phrases, and I don't know who was more surprised, me or the cat.

'Roll over tickle tummy.'

I saw a second of confusion in the dancer's eyes, then a smile, then a flip; she was on her back with all four 'legs' in the air and Lourdes was tickling her tummy. Lourdes had learned the expression when Stephen's son, Ben, was teaching Domingo to do exactly that trick. I had never thought that she would find the opportunity to use it, especially in a London theatre. During the next enchanting hour, we had four more visits; one of the cats even sat on her lap and, ignoring her giggles completely, proceeded to extend a back leg and wash itself.

Like most good times, it was over too quickly, and there was a well-deserved standing ovation following two encores. Then, as we were preparing to leave, six of the dancers ran to the front of the stage and, as one, pointed long, slim, elegant arms at Lourdes, clapped and blew kisses. She leapt to her feet and returned both affections.

What a wonderful day. We walked south, back through Covent Garden. Eleven o'clock and all the theatres were emptying: it was rush hour in show land, and taxis were hard to find. When we reached the Strand, I decided that the junction with the Aldwych was probably our best bet. Standing on that corner, I explained to Lourdes that it might take a while to find a cab. Having spent more time in taxis in the last 48 hours than she ever had in her life, she was happy to wait and just watch the world go by.

A young man approached and waved a cigarette at us, wordlessly asking for a light. I smoke. I have managed to give up the patches and the chewing gum, but not the fags. My only rule is that I don't smoke in the street. Ever. My conversation with Lourdes was, of course, in Spanish, and, having overheard it, he probably thought he was dealing with a couple of vulnerable tourists.

'Sorry, I don't have a lighter.'

My response to his request, in unaccented English, obviously threw him for a moment, but not for long. He took two steps back, smiled, then proceeded to light his cigarette from matches produced from his pocket. He stood there staring at us. I didn't like it; it smelled like trouble. Lourdes picked up on the tension.

'Lourdes, let's walk. There don't seem to be any taxis coming up here.'

We walked, quickly, arm in arm. He followed, too closely behind, and within seconds was joined by another man.

'Buy us a drink, girls.'

Ignoring him seemed to make him angry. He tapped me on the shoulder from behind, then again, but much harder. The Strand was still busy, but I was beginning to get scared. Suddenly they were both in front of us: they stopped, forcing us to do the same.

'Give us your money. Right now.'

It wasn't worth getting hurt or ruining our break, that was for sure, but I was as angry as I was scared. Over their shoulders, I could see the two doormen from the Savoy Hotel flagging down taxis, no more than ten yards ahead. Clutching Lourdes close and hard, I pushed past and almost frogmarched her into the hotel entrance. The two men stayed on the street, one of them calling obscenities. We were safe, but, had we been two Spanish tourists, I'm not at all sure that we would have been.

Where it all began: the hamlet of La Molineta
with Casa Rosa and La Panificadora.

Number One Dog, Charly,
making Minstral, a foster kitten,
feel safe and welcome

Domingo, a small dog with a big ego and an even bigger heart.

Charly listens and Niña has a cuddle
as I tell them about that year's *feria*.

Lourdes. Just look at the warmth that she radiates.

Tintin, Domingo, Charly and Niña in the window
of La Panificadora, all wearing their usual
'Why did you leave us?' expressions.

Stephen walking Tintin at sunset
in September on the 'crowded
beaches of the Costa del Sol'.

Javier, Rosario and our
godchildren,
Claudia and Nicolas.

We educate our animals well.
Claudia at her
flower-arranging class.

Typically terrified puppies:
Babe and her brother Piglet about
an hour after we found them.

Claudia's son William, my long-awaited tabby,
with blind boy Radar and Tilly.

Frigiliana: following Mass, the procession
is blessed before parading through the village.

Fiesta frills: picnicking under the pines at
feria, the fiesta for San Antonio.

'Big Bear' or 'Square Bear', our Ocho weighs more than me.

Tilly Todd. Enough said.

Stephen with Antonio outside the bar in La Molineta.

2007's Christmas hamper. Cracker with Santa.
Pudding and sister Holly were close by.

Cracker, still a baby, loves playing the role of big brother.
Pictured here with Biggles, a cream pup with wrinkly caramel
ears that looked like an old leather flying helmet.

30

Inbound

So soon, it was time to leave, and for Lourdes that meant many more long goodbyes. Goodbye to the receptionists, the doorman, the porter, the girl from Galicia serving breakfasts. Goodbye to the Filipino cleaning lady, who certainly wouldn't have too much to do in Lourdes's room. When I went to collect her, the shrine had been repacked, the bed was stripped, the used linen and towels folded neatly and placed on a chair, and she was lamenting the fact that that she couldn't find any bleach to clean her bathroom.

We left our luggage with reception and set off for our final couple of hours in the city. It was raining yet again. On day one, I had cautioned Lourdes against buying the first things she saw as presents for her family; consequently, we now had to retrace many of our steps to pick up the 'must-have' items. So again we were close to Piccadilly when I remembered my promise to an old friend in the village to bring back her favourite breakfast tea from Fortnum's, their own blend.

In hindsight, I suppose, explaining to Lourdes that I had to go to a food shop to buy some tea for a friend didn't really prepare her for Fortnum & Mason's food hall. As ever, it could have been a stage set – though certainly not from *Cats* – as everything was presented so beautifully. The theme of the moment was peacocks; in the centre of every display, the stuffed birds were there, with tails dropped and spread, or fanned like rainbows above their heads.

'Jackie, this is a shop? Yes?'

'Yes, Lourdes. I'm buying some tea.'

'This is a shop? A food shop? Can you buy these birds to eat?'

'No, they are for decoration, they are dead and stuffed, just like the heads of the mountain goats in the village bar.'

'How sad that we cannot take a photograph, I would love to show my family what food shops look like in London.'

OK. Fortnum & Mason's food hall is not exactly your average Spar or even Sainsbury's, but the idea that Lourdes could have a photo of this and explain to her village that it was a London food shop amused me enormously. I went over to one of the many assistants, all dressed in pinstriped trousers and frock coats.

'Excuse me.'

'Madam?'

'Would there be any problem if I took a photograph of my friend in front of one of the displays? It is her first time in London, and she would like a photo.'

'Madam, Fortnum's would be honoured. May I suggest, should you permit me to use your camera, that I take one of you both?'

Learn a lesson M&S!

The taxi driver that we hailed in Piccadilly was delighted to learn that we wanted to go to Heathrow via our hotel in Lancaster Gate: it was the middle of the day, the traffic was heavy, much better to get out of town, it was a good fare. He talked non-stop. When Lourdes asked me if I knew all the taxi drivers in London, I was stumped. I didn't know any, then I realised that in Spain, the land where everyone talks to each other, taxi drivers are the exception: they don't talk, they just drive, very, very fast. In England, certainly in London, it is usually the reverse.

Heathrow, and with amazing luck, we managed to find that very same trolley and weaved an unsteady course to the Iberia check-in desk. I presented the tickets, the passports and prepared myself for the usual questions.

'Is this your baggage?'

'Yes.'

'Did you pack it yourself?'

'Yes.'

The usual, but for Lourdes it was official and therefore important. I was standing there nodding and shaking at the right moments and idly wondering that if I were a suicide bomber, would I behave or answer any differently? Then came the big question.

'Are you carrying anything for anyone else?'

'Yes, many, many things.'

I snapped out of my stupor.

'*No*. Lourdes, *no*. You are not carrying anything for anyone else.'

The check-in girl raised a pencilled-in eyebrow.

'But I am, Jackie, I am. Remember, for my mother I bought a cardigan; I wanted it in blue, but they didn't have her size so I bought the green, but still I think she will like it. For my father a shirt; it is always difficult to know what to get him. It was difficult to decide what to get for my sisters, too, there was so much choice, but in the end they both have scarves and tea towels.' She turned back to the girl behind the desk. 'Carmina's has a picture of the Big Bin, the clock, and Aurora's has the Queen's horses in her corral. Aurora's three children have toys; no, that's not true, for Eva, in the end, I bought a hair slide, she is ten and too old for toys, and for Aurora's husband . . .'

She gave a three- or four-minute monologue, the queue behind was backing up impatiently and yet the check-in girl was enchanted and seemed suddenly to be in no hurry. It was established that Lydia was from Asturias and had never been to

Andalucía, although her parents had visited friends there, and that Lourdes had never been to Asturias and didn't even know anyone who had. Finally, we got our boarding cards. With a delay and therefore over two hours' wait in the departure lounge, Lourdes reaped yet more freebies, this time mainly miniatures of whiskies and brandies (shame she doesn't drink).

At the boarding gate, we were asked to stand aside for a moment, then told that we had been upgraded to club class. It could only have been the work of Lydia, the girl at check-in. I was delighted: it meant more space and free cava all the way home. Lourdes, whose charm, I was sure, had achieved this upgrade, was totally oblivious.

31

Home

An onlooker at Málaga Airport that evening would have been forgiven for thinking that Lourdes was meeting her long-lost husband and had her friend in tow. She launched herself at Stephen from a distance of at least three feet and, having applied a serious layer of one of her sample lipsticks in the ladies' while we waited for our luggage, by the time I caught up he looked stunned and rouged.

'Lourdes. Did you enjoy London?'

'Stephen. I do not have the words to tell you everything that I have seen.'

For the next hour she found the words, millions of them, she didn't stop describing with fresh eyes and voice the things that I had taken for granted for years, and with a memory for detail that was stunning. Although our flight had been delayed by two hours, when we arrived in the village just after midnight, all her family and friends were in the street outside her house waiting for her. It was as if time had stood still. There were many tears of joy from the women and blessings for her safe return. Her father enquired about what it had been like to be so near to the clouds; at this, Lourdes just looked over her shoulder, smiled and winked at us.

It's oh-so-nice to go travelling, but oh-so-nice to come home, or words to that effect, and how true. Stephen indulged my euphoria.

'You've lost weight.'

'I don't think so.'

'The dogs have forgotten me.'

'No, they haven't.'

'Everything in the garden has grown enormously.'

'Really?'

'It's much hotter than when I left.'

'That was three days ago.'

'Not making sense, am I?'

'Not really, and I haven't got a word in edgeways.'

'It's just so good to be home.'

If Stephen starts a sentence with 'I've got something to tell you . . .', then I know it is something important.

'I've got something to tell you . . .'

I already knew the first part of the story. Stephen had played golf a couple of weeks before and caught up with the people in front of his group. They were loading a young cat into a pet carrier on the back of their buggy. The woman explained that she had been watching it for several days and, with its teats full of milk, had thought there must be kittens close by. Despite a thorough search, no kittens had been found, and the young mum needed a lot of TLC. I'll fast forward a bit here; the lady adopted the cat, it settled in well and was taken to have the operation that would ensure a few less homeless kitties would be produced in the future. Six days later, in almost the same place, two very hungry kittens were found. There were empty cat-food sachets scattered around, so people had obviously been feeding them, but they were filthy and dehydrated. The kittens closely resembled their mother and, looking forward to a happy family reunion, the same kind lady decided that there was room in her heart and space in her house for two more. Nice idea, but it didn't work. As we have discovered, neutered females rarely like their own kittens. Once the vet has dealt with the medical bits, a switch seems to flick in their brain that turns them into the mothers from hell.

'So, where are they now?'

'In the little bedroom.'

'Would that be *our* little bedroom by any chance?'

Purring so hard that the bed rattled, looking clean, fit and fluffy, were our two new little girls. They were no more than a month old: a classic black-and-white and her sister, who had been blessed with strong ginger splodges too. We decided that they deserved brave names, having spent a week alone without their mum. They are Thelma and Louise.

32

Sevillana Dances and Dresses

By the time we got back from London, *feria*, the annual festival of San Antonio, was less than a month away. For the previous two years, I had watched enviously as the village women and men, who by then we knew so well, swirled around each other in the beautiful four-part dance called *sevillana*. It originates from the time when, at festivals, the girls approaching marriageable age, normally kept securely behind the *rejas* (iron-barred windows) of their houses, would be allowed to attend dances during fiestas. Watched, especially by their families but also by the whole village, these courting couples would dance as close to each other as possible, but were never allowed to touch. The result is a dance far steamier than anything seen in today's discos.

I was literally stuffed into a prickly pink tutu at the age of three by an over-ambitious mother. I then, with little talent, endured tap, ballet, ballroom and Latin American lessons, together with a brief, disastrous flirtation with gymnastics. It is therefore really rather surprising that I still love dancing, but I do.

So, when Lourdes had suggested, the previous February, that I join the *sevillana* class starting that week in the village hall, I jumped at the chance. She would come with me, she said, it was a long time since she had learned and the practice would do her good.

Bless her, she was born to dance and certainly didn't need the practice, but I was the only foreigner in a class of 20 and very grateful for her company and support.

Remember the rub-your-tummy-and-pat-your-head-at-the-same-time trick when you were a kid? This is *sevillana*. To begin with, there is a lot more intricate foot work than in classical English dance, but it doesn't stop there. After the first lesson, I felt quite proud of my grasp of things, after the second, positively cocky, but then came the arms.

'Reach up to pick an apple, eat it and throw it away.'

'What?'

While your feet are doing Fred Astaire proud, you also have to produce creative windmills with your arms. The action is likened to reaching out to pick an apple from a tree, pulling it towards you to eat, and then, with an underarm, backwards movement, throwing away the core. By the end of lesson ten, and the fourth and final part of the dance, the feet were doing quite well, but the arms still had a long way to go. Lourdes was touchingly pleased with my progress and pronounced that I was ready to dance at that year's fiesta.

About ten days before fiesta week, the flamenco dresses arrive from Sevilla at Encarnación's shop in the village. She normally sells between ten and twenty dresses a year, but each one is tried on by at least fifty village women, who have no intention of buying; it is just part of the ritual and excitement in the build-up to the event and accepted as such. The dresses are deceptively heavy, and cleverly designed to be altered with ease. The inside seams have a good three inches of excess material, allowing a size twelve to become a ten or a fourteen with a little needlework.

I was summoned by Lourdes to meet her at seven that evening outside the village's only clothes shop. Outside was a good idea. Inside were 30 or more women, teenage girls and children in varying states of undress. These dresses are perfect for the Spanish figure, which, in general, tends to be small on top and

– there is no way to put this politely – enormous around the
bum. They cling down to the waist or just below, and then flare
and ruffle, hiding a multitude of sins and cellulite. The bodices
are tightly fitted and the backs dive almost to the waist; therefore
wearing a bra, at least one that you can buy around here, is out
of the question.

When my turn came, at least an hour later, I chose two
dresses, almost second-hand by that stage, and headed towards
the changing cubicle. Lourdes and her sisters came with me,
carrying two dresses apiece, though for them there was no
intention of buying. In the space of the average toilet cubicle,
the four of us stripped to our knickers and wriggled into yards
of heavy frills.

I had spotted the dress that I wanted the moment I arrived in
front of the shop: it was a deep, rich blue, almost navy, with tiny
red, white and yellow flowers embroidered on the three layers of
frills. At the time it was on a dummy in the window – but not
for long. It was the perfect length, but far too tight on top and
far too big around the hips. I was more than a little disappointed
and about to take it off when, as usual, Lourdes took over. From
behind me, she reached into the front of the dress and, without
ceremony, repositioned my boobs, the left more left and higher,
same on the right. She called for Encarnación's mother, the
seamstress, Concepción. Of course, the name has a different,
more religious meaning here, but I do still have a problem with
the idea of calling your baby daughter after the biological process
that preceded her arrival. Concepción, through a mouth full of
pins, declared to the whole shop that it was the first time in her
65 years that she had been required to let a dress *out* at the top
and take it *in* at the bottom. They all came to look and I felt like
the star attraction at the freak show, but when she had finished,
it fitted perfectly, and the past pleasures of my Armani business
suits or my Aquascutum cashmere coat paled in comparison. At
that year's *feria*, I danced till I dropped.

33

Tintin

'How was the golf?'

Silly question, really. By the time he had carelessly parked the car, slammed the boot, slung the clubs into the basement and stomped up the steps, even the dogs knew the answer to that one. After a very brief single wag of low-tails greeting, Charly, Domingo and Niña made a wise and swift retreat to their baskets, heads down. Time to change the subject.

'Remember the dog I told you about; it's been around on and off for at least a few weeks now. The one that looks like the dog in the *Tintin* cartoons. What was the name of the dog in the *Tintin* cartoons? Well, anyway, today it was back again and it looks worse than ever, really sad and thin. It has no road sense; cars have been swerving to avoid it. But it won't last long out there.'

'We have more than enough dogs,' Stephen replied.

'Of course we do. I wasn't suggesting that we take it in.'

'Good.'

Rubbish collection is pretty efficient around here – because of the heat, it has to be. There are wheelie bins at the edge of every cluster of houses, which are emptied every night. Ours was three minutes' walk away, up past Antonio's bar; Stephen made a nightly pilgrimage. That night, standing at the kitchen sink, looking out of the window, with my very poor long-distance

sight, it seemed to me that Stephen was bringing the rubbish back again. He was definitely carrying something white.

'It's the Tintin dog I've been telling you about. Where did you find him?'

'Lying under the rubbish bins. He's so, so thin, almost starved, and he can't stop shivering. I couldn't just leave him out there.'

'No, of course you couldn't, but Stephen, we don't need any more dogs.'

I just couldn't resist the chance to turn the verbal tables.

By this stage, we were relatively well practised in the art of introducing a new animal to the pack. Stephen sat on the floor in the corner inside our front door with the Tintin dog in his arms, and the other three came and had a good sniff until they were satisfied that there was no threat. In this case, we felt that it was especially important that he was introduced to the others gently. He was in such a poor way: pitifully thin, almost bald, terrified of everything, and Stephen had the slightly soggy trousers to prove it. We need not have worried; it was immediately obvious to our three that this excuse for a dog couldn't fight its way out of a paper bag.

Yet more radio appeals and vet visits. In Rafael's waiting room the following day, Stephen spotted a cut on the dog's front leg that had been stitched. Rafael said that he hadn't done it; he would have certainly remembered such a strange-looking animal. A tour of the town's veterinary practices gave us the answer. His name was Loopy. The Danish vet had stitched him several times recently when he had been brought in by various strangers who had clipped him with their cars. He gave us the mobile-phone number for his German owner, and Stephen made the call.

'Hello, I believe we have found your dog. White, with huge black ears. Loopy?'

'It iss not my dog. I do not vaunt zee dog. Go see my ex-husband.'

She gave the address, then the line went dead.

We went to the house every day for the next two weeks, but there was never anyone there. The note we had pushed under the gate had gone, but we had not had a call, and meanwhile we were both becoming very attached to Loopy, or Tintin, as we called him.

He had more or less stopped trembling when we got close to him and was very subservient with the other three dogs, rolling on his back, avoiding eye contact and curling his tail under him whenever they approached. For the first week, he ate and slept, ate and slept, then he slept, curled into a tight ball, and ate. As he became more relaxed, we nicknamed him Flatpack. He was so thin that when lying on his side, he looked like a cheap IKEA bookcase or wardrobe waiting to be assembled.

Back to the supposed dog-owner's house for what must have been the twentieth visit, and this time a man in his early thirties with long, mousy, greasy hair answered the door.

'Hello. I believe we have found your dog, white with huge black ears. Loopy? Look, we have him here, now, in our car.'

'It iss not my dog. It belongs to my ex-vife.'

'Yes. Well, actually, we have spoken to her, and she says that she doesn't want him, she says that he is yours.'

'In zat case, I s'pose I muss bring it in.'

Stephen and I took one look at each other and then, without a word between us, yet in unison:

'We'll keep him. If you really don't want him, that is.'

'Gutt. Zank you. Guttbye.'

When he shut the door without a second glance at Tintin, or any enquiry as to our ability to care for him, we knew we had done the right thing. After all, we had three dogs; one more wouldn't make much difference – or so we tried to convince ourselves.

In the first six months, he didn't put on much weight; in truth, he never really has. He has filled out a little in the hollows between his ribs and, from being almost bald, his wiry coat has grown thick and shiny. Best of all, he will now look us in the eye, wag his tail with such joy as to swipe two coffee cups to the floor in one go and fall asleep on his back with all four legs in the air.

It is amusing to us that so many of our English visitors enquire about the breeds of our brood. There seems to be an obsession with pedigree, which, in my opinion, is responsible for many of the Bride of Frankenstein animals that the Kennel Club seems to promote and prize so dearly. In Tintin's case, many people say lurcher, then pause and add that it could be a very, very hairy greyhound. White, with bat-like black ears and a big black patch on his back, the rims to his eyes are pink. Until his fur grew, with his spotted skin he looked like a very thin, bald Dalmatian. If I were to choose an actor to play him in a movie, it would have to be Donald Sutherland in his role in *Kelly's Heroes*, and I have been very tempted to buy him the leather flying helmet. We have already decided that Elizabeth Hurley gets the part of Niña. She's a good actress and would look great in a black dress held together by safety pins (Niña, that is). The jury is still out on the other two, although Charlton Heston is on the shortlist for Charly's role, and Mickey Rooney would have done a good Domingo.

A month or so later, we were sitting in companionable silence on the terrace late one evening, staring up at a clear, starry sky, with the four dogs at our feet, when Stephen did it again:

'Snowy.'

'You have got to be joking. It's August, and anyway it never gets anywhere near freezing point here.'

'Snowy. The dog in the *Tintin* cartoons was called Snowy.'

34

Do You Play Golf Too?

August, the month of madness. Everywhere is full: the hotels, the shops, the restaurants and the beaches. Many tourists drop what was a dubious dress code to begin with and wander around the town sporting Speedos, beer bellies and bum bags. Last summer, I gave thanks that at least the man walking towards me was wearing a white singlet, until, up closer, I realised that that must have been yesterday: he was naked from the waist up and seriously sunburned. The queue at the bank's foreign-exchange counter stretched out of the door, even longer than usual. Eventually, the woman at the head of the queue turned to the people behind her and announced in a very loud voice, 'I don't know what all the fuss is about. Just because when they asked me at home where I was going and I said France, they went and gave me the wrong traveller's cheques. Now, here, they are making a big fuss about it.'

One reason to be thankful for the euro!

Michael, my hairdresser, called one morning to ask if any of our houses were empty. In August? Silly question, Michael. He went on to explain that the man having his hair cut at that moment had arrived in Nerja the night before with his wife and daughter. That they were here for four days to look at the possibility of designing a golf course, and the only flight out of Dublin at short notice had been a cheap package. They had taken it, assuming that they could move to a better hotel or rent a villa when they arrived. In August! I knew where they were staying and felt sorry for them. I promised to make some calls and get back to him within a few minutes, which I did, but only to report that as I had expected, everywhere I could possibly think of was full. I was about to put the phone down when something funny came over me; to this day, I don't know why I did what I did.

When Stephen and I had first talked seriously about living in Spain, we had discussed creating an exclusive bed-and-breakfast place. It was only a thought, and a daft one at that, luckily quickly dismissed. Stephen likes his privacy and I hate cooking breakfast before midday, not exactly the right credentials.

'Michael, if they are really stuck, I suppose we could put them up on a sort of bed-and-breakfast basis. I've never done it before, and we have four dogs now: that might be a problem, especially with a child. Ask him, and do explain that I have never done this before. If he is interested, he can come up and have a look, then decide.'

'I'm giving him directions; they will be with you in 20 minutes.'

Christy and the two Annes, his wife and daughter, arrived and introduced themselves. As charming as only the Irish can be, they pronounced the bedrooms and bathrooms perfect, had no problem with the fact that I was new to this sort of thing, said they only ever had coffee and toast for breakfast anyway and fell in love with the dogs. They went back to the coast to pack and were installed within the hour, with instructions to make themselves at home. They had a swim, and we all sat on the terrace with a bottle of chilled white wine.

'Michael said that you were here to look at the possibility of designing a new golf course. Do you play too?'

'I have been known to.'

'That's where Stephen is now, playing golf, he should be back any minute.'

I heard the car pull up and went to explain our new state; it didn't seem fair to let him just walk in on strangers.

'Darling, how was the golf? Ummm, we have people staying with us.'

'People?'

'Only for three nights.'

'People. For three nights.'

I explained Michael's phone call and my rather less explicable reaction to it.

'They are very nice. He is here to look at designing a golf course; you'll find that interesting, won't you? Anyway come and meet them, the wife and daughter are both called Anne, and he is Christy something, Connor, I think.'

I was babbling.

'Christy? Irish? Here to look at designing a golf course.'

'Yes.'

'Christy O'Connor?'

'I think so, yes.'

'Christy O'Connor Jnr.'

'No, no. He doesn't look very junior.'

'Do you know who Christy O'Connor is? His shot basically won the '89 Ryder Cup, playing with Cañizares, a two iron if I remember rightly, to within four or five feet of the pin. People still talk about it.'

'Well, I'm sure he's not the same one, but he did say that he played some golf.'

He was the same one. They stayed with us for three nights, one of which we spent in Antonio's bar. Antonio was on particularly good form, clapping the hollow-handed clap of the local *cante jondo*, with the accompaniment from Aurelio of a slow beat of his walking stick. (For Stephen and me, an animated Aurelio was a new experience. Every day he hobbled down from the village and spent three or four hours nursing a glass of red wine in his little corner of the bar. He rarely spoke, often dozed, then retraced his steps home before sunset.) Christy picked up two teaspoons and joined them; they were delighted to learn a new form of peasant folk music. At three in the morning, I pointed out it was getting late and got the Irish response that 'the man who made time made plenty of it'. I translated for Antonio and discovered that the Spanish have exactly the same expression, and they also 'touch wood' and avoid walking under ladders.

'I wouldn't be minding nine holes in the morning, it would be doing me arm good. Would you be interested?'

Stephen went pale. He had been playing for less than a year and had a handicap of about 180. Gamely he agreed, thoroughly enjoyed their half round and Christy taught him a lot. When they left, promising to return soon, Stephen asked me if I had charged them for their stay.

'Of course, that was the agreement.'

'Don't you realise that I would have paid ten times that just to have met, let alone have had a game with, Christy O'Connor.'

Golfers.

35

Casa Carolina

About a third of the way through the project in Maro, Juan, our lawyer, had called to ask if we would be interested in buying a house about half a mile from us. Stephen had chosen Juan for his legal skills and experience. I approved because he was the most elegant, charming, old-fashioned Spanish gentleman I had ever met. He acted for the elderly English owners who were finding the house too much for them, but having lived there every winter for 30 years they wanted a quick, quiet, no-fuss sale. Our first Antonio, now a friend, whom we met when buying Casa Rosa, has one of the town's largest estate agents and bemoans the fact that when it rains and the tourists can't hit the beaches, many of them hit the agencies to occupy their day viewing houses with little or no intention of buying. This was exactly what these people were trying to avoid.

We agreed, though with little enthusiasm, to have a look and arranged to meet Juan there later that morning, although with work in Maro going full steam ahead, we both felt that we had enough on our plates at the time. The house was exactly what you would expect from an elderly couple after 30 years of habitation: much too much furniture, lots of dark-brown, heavily varnished wood, beige walls and pink upholstery. Like the owners themselves, it was looking rather tired. The price they were asking was more than fair and reflected the fact that they didn't have a pool, although the large garden, their pride and joy, was stunning. We made the usual polite 'we-will-think-about-it' noises and left. Ten minutes later, Juan was at our door offering the house at a reduced price, with the typically Spanish explanation that 'they likes you'.

Still we said no and forgot about it for more than a month. At least I forgot about it.

'We should have gone for it, you know, we were stupid,' said Stephen.

'Gone for what?'

'That house. Casa Carolina. It wouldn't have taken a lot to change it around, new floors and doors, paint everything white and we would have had to put in a pool, of course. Then, if we moved the entrance so that people arrived from the little lane below and walked up through the gardens past all the fruit trees, which would be rather lovely, we could have shut the existing entrance off and still have more than enough land to build another house.'

Even to me, this not only stacked up, it also became quite an intriguing proposition. An empty plot where we could design from scratch: what an adventure. *Parcelas* (building plots) in that area were selling for almost as much as they were asking for the house. We agreed that the following morning Stephen would call on Juan to see if it was still on the market, though we doubted it very much. Early next morning, before Stephen left for town, Juan called us again with his final offer. We bit his hand off.

We had brazenly and obviously fallen in love with Casa Rosa and then with La Panificadora, and paid the asking price for both. It just goes to prove that appearing not to be interested can be the best form of negotiation, though that was not, in this case, our original intention.

36

Surprise, Surprise

Lourdes's birthday is on 21 July. Every year we now have a 'women-and-children-only' pool party. The first of these, a year after we moved here permanently, was a surprise. She had left as usual at two on Tuesday, saying that she would see us on Friday, if not before. It was only later that afternoon I realised that Friday was her birthday. I called her sisters and we made plans. The joy of July, like May, June, August and September, is that you can guarantee that the weather will be fine and outdoor eating can be planned in advance.

Friday. Lourdes arrived wearing her usual smile and Lycra, and we chatted over our coffee cups, yet she appeared a little quieter than usual. I, of course, knew that she was disappointed that I had forgotten her birthday, but that she was determined not to mention it. I busied myself in the kitchen, cooking two huge paellas, laying out plates of *jamón* and chorizo, preparing salads, roasting peppers and making pizzas for the children. She walked onto the terrace as I was stacking plates, and I explained that I had invited friends to come to lunch.

She would finish as usual at two and, as arranged, her sisters, her son and her best friends, together with their children, began to arrive just before. It was difficult to smuggle nine women, three of them heavily pregnant, and fourteen children into the kitchen without attracting her attention, but with much giggling and shushing we managed it.

'Lourdes, could you come here for a moment please.'

The doors to the kitchen were shut. I pointed in their direction with a nervous look and explained that there was a funny noise in there. In a year, she had become used to my overreactions to the birds, mice, occasionally rats, gigantic geckos and huge spiders that come into the house and are part of day-to-day life here. Rolling up her sleeves, she pushed the doors open with an air of authority, prepared to take on whatever it was. But she was not prepared for what she encountered.

'*¡Feliz cumpleaños!*'

'Happy birthday to you!'

It took us all at least five minutes to stop her crying. We had a wonderful afternoon. The children turned into happy prunes after many hours in the pool, and my Spanish vocabulary increased, richly surrounded by the local gossip.

Since then the party has grown. The three 'bumps' that bounced around the pool that year all now have little brothers or sisters. Last year it was sixteen women, and only one with a bump – Carmina, Lourdes's little sister, was finally pregnant – and twenty-three children. On these occasions, Stephen is always packed off to the mountains, much to his relief. He takes the dogs, his favourite sandwiches, a good book and a golf club. He stands on a crest of land with a big bag of old golf balls beside him and hits them into our valley below. This serves two purposes: he assures me it helps to improve his swing, and the dogs have great fun and exercise chasing after the balls, though they very rarely bring them back. As one of our dog books advised: if you want a dog that retrieves, buy a retriever. But for all the varied genes that our lot must possess, I don't think there is one retriever gene amongst them.

I was an only child, and my best friend had six brothers and sisters. We envied each other. When she took her school report home, it was one of many, good or bad; mine was the sole focus of attention. However my ten out of ten was celebrated, her achievement could be lost as one of seven. It is the same with the dogs: one out of four, at any given moment, is in a degree of disgrace. At the *cortijo*, it is almost always Domingo, the motorbike chaser. He hears them coming from way down the track, and unless we are quick enough to lunge at his collar, he is off. In contrast, indoors, he is an angel.

37

Back to Work

The full heat of the summer was fading, and it was time to look seriously at getting Casa Carolina ready for the following year. Replace the tired terrazzo floors with terracotta tiles. Strip all the dark and heavily varnished woodwork and paint it white. This takes seconds to write, but days of nail- and back-breaking work to achieve. Change the heavy doors for the half glazed variety to double the amount of light entering the house. Retile both bathrooms; those Barbie pinks had to go. Where to put the pool?

The garden was large and mature. Wherever we dug, it would, sadly, mean losing at least two prime trees. For a week, we went there every day at different times: with oranges and a flask of fresh coffee for breakfast at seven thirty in the morning, a time that Stephen found especially productive because I didn't speak; lunchtimes with sandwiches; evenings with a bottle of wine. It was a luxury to be able to do this before making any major decisions and has paid such dividends. The pool and summerhouse that we built are in exactly the right place to take maximum advantage of the long hours of sunshine that bless the garden, with views to sea and mountains that are spectacular.

With the house, we also inherited another Antonio: the 73-year-old 'Antonio *de dos dientes*'. *Dientes* are teeth, and he is the proud owner of two in a fetching shade of saffron yellow: one at the top, one at the bottom, though, inconveniently, they are on opposite sides of his mouth.

Like many of the older men in the village, he has an accent as thick as treacle. I understand roughly one word in four. He has been Carolina's gardener for more than 35 years; it is his second home, he knows every plant, every tree, every stone. We have put visitors' books in every house, and Antonio gets more favourable mentions than the Alhambra Palace.

We have been told that when we bought the house he feared he would lose his job. It wasn't the loss of income that worried him – he was paid for only four hours a week but spent more than four hours a day there – it was the idea that it may no longer be his garden. Stephen has since promised him that he will have the job for as long as he wants it and that he can be buried there if he chooses, a suggestion which delights him and I truly hope he doesn't hold us to.

38

The *Cortijo*

Over a period of about two and a half years – the first two and a half years of our retirement! – we had moved from Casa Rosa to La Panificadora, bought the little house in Maro and built it up from its ruins, then done a total makeover of Casa Carolina. While we were finishing work on that, Paco, our builder, always keen to do the odd deal on the side, asked Stephen to go and look at a plot of land that his friend was selling about 20 minutes' drive above the village. He thought Stephen might find it interesting. Stephen did.

We had been watching the incredible increase in the price of property and land around here, and were pretty sure that if we could buy the right place at the right price, just sit on it for a few years and then sell on, we would be improving our returns. Luckily, it seems that we have been right: 13,000 square metres of land with an existing small *cortijo*, a small cottage. It has piped water from a well, rumoured to have never run dry, but no electricity. We call it the world's most expensive private picnic site because that, so far, is all we have ever really used it for.

We go there and let the dogs run; it is very rare that a car goes past. Only three or four minutes' drive down a dirt track off the only road that rises from Frigiliana and although less than half an hour's drive away from home, it is considerably higher than where we live and, therefore, in summer, much cooler.

The lack of electricity is actually a bonus: as the daylight fades, we light candles and enjoy the mood that only candlelight can provide. It has already provided the site for some of the best days of my life, sitting picnicking with friends in our overgrown meadows, full of wild flowers and trees laden with figs, lemons, olives and pomegranates, looking down on the gleaming white village dwarfed by the mountains, the Sierras (the Saws), that tower jaggedly above it and watching the trans-African ferries on the distant Mediterranean horizon.

That winter, on one of the lost days between Christmas and Día de los Reyes on 6 January, the sun was bright, though the air was cool. We wrapped up, relatively speaking, in long trousers and fleeces, and along with the turkey-and-stuffing sandwiches we packed our books, our four dogs and a bottle of wine into the car and spent a peaceful afternoon at the *cortijo* enjoying just that: our books, our dogs, our sandwiches, the wine, the peace and the views. Driving home at dusk, we slowed to allow the last few goats of the herd to cross the road in front of us and looked out for Julio. We are used to seeing them around; Julio, Lourdes's husband, has his corral only 15 minutes away from our *cortijo*, and we always put a bottle of beer in the coolbox alongside our wine for when we met him in the mountains.

This day, however, it was Julio Pequeño (Little Julio, the son) who was walking the herd, something he was very used to. But today he was more than busy, throwing stones to try and contain three hundred dumb (and goats make sheep look bright) animals, while one of their number was in the process of giving birth by the side of the road. He was kneeling beside it.

'*Hola*. Julio, can we help?'

'Stephen. Yes please, she is a first time mother and not doing that well, the baby has started early.'

With a calm wisdom and experience well beyond his 14 years, he took charge. The mum to be was lying on her side, bleating furiously.

'Hold her tight under the forelegs as tight as you can with both arms. Just don't let go, and keep your face away; she is normally very sweet, but right now she may bite.'

I was standing at the 'working end' and could see that both back legs had already arrived. Julio took both tiny legs in one hand and put his other on the mother's stomach, waiting for two or three minutes, then, as it contracted, he pulled very smoothly and gently, and one of the first goats of the new millennium spewed into view.

'It's a boy.'

The mother was on her feet within seconds; she bit through the cord and started to walk away. It was an impressive recovery, but more than a little short on bonding. We both stood there being useless, until Julio threw a rope at Stephen and told him to keep the mother there. He sat with the newborn in his lap and, putting his face to its mouth, sucked and spat three times. Grabbing the reluctant mother, he used considerable force, a sort of rugby tackle, to lay her on her side and kneaded a teat until it produced the milk that the little one so desperately needed. Bright kid, it caught on straight away and began guzzling greedily, but within a couple of minutes the mother had again had enough. She stood up, literally shook the baby off the teat and walked towards the rest of the herd without a backward glance.

'Stephen, would you mind taking the new one back to the corral? My grandfather is there; he will look after it. We have to be out for at least another hour; of course, I can carry it, but he would be better in the warm.'

'What about the mother?'

'Oh, she's fine, she will walk with us.'

I was incensed. No wonder she was so pissed off: where was the champagne, the bouquets of flowers, the phone calls, the telegrams, the presents and the visitors? When was she going to have her warm aromatherapy bath and change into her new, carefully chosen nightie, ready to hold court and look serene? After all she had just been through, she got to go for a walk.

I wrapped the baby in Stephen's favourite cashmere jumper, which was lying on the back seat (something he has never quite forgiven me for, although the stains did come out eventually). We drove to the corral and handed him over to the *abuelo* (grandfather), and therein lies another story.

The previous spring, a wart had appeared on the middle finger of my left hand. Some people are warty, but I never had been: it was my first, and I hated it. It sat on the next finger to the beautiful emerald-and-diamond ring that Stephen had given me many years before. It grew rapidly, was soon competing with the diamonds and, despite every remedy that was recommended, including something called 'Bazuka' sent from England, it looked like it was there to stay. When this thing was in its infancy, Lourdes casually mentioned that I should go and see her father-in-law, who was famous in the village for getting rid of warts: he only had to touch someone and their wart was gone. By this time it was competing with the Leaning Tower of Pisa, and I was almost desperate enough to chase a bit of witchcraft. Within two days of handing the newborn kid over to Lourdes's father-in-law, just as one would pass a small baby, the wart had halved in size. Within a week it had disappeared, and when I told Lourdes about it, she simply replied, 'Of course.'

39

Javier and Rosario

We were just finishing our meal at Las Chinas, a popular restaurant in the village, where Sebastian serves a fish soup rivalling anything you could find in France. This is not the Chinese restaurant it is often mistaken for. *Chinas* are the smooth pebbles used to pave the streets, a form of uneven natural cobblestones. At the next table, a couple with a sleeping baby had arrived after us and, as is usual here, and a custom we find charming, before sitting down they had nodded and wished us '*que aproveche*' ('enjoy your meal').

'Timing is everything,' they say. With the timing that only small babies can perfect, as their plates were put in front of them, she woke and began to cry. She was not to be ignored. Both mother and father tried to humour and jolly her on shoulders and laps while their food began to go cold, and she just got louder and louder. This is where my interfering bit kicks in. Stephen hates it. I love small babies, and it seemed silly for me not to take her and let them enjoy their meal, though it is most certainly an offer I would no longer make in England. Years later, they teased me about my Spanish in those days, claiming that what I said was 'me baby take'. They passed her over with a smile; I managed to calm her, allowing them to finish their meal in peace. That was our first meeting with Javier, Rosario and their exquisite baby daughter, Claudia. Although we had never met them before, they, like 90 per cent of the village, knew who we were, where we lived and that I had taken Lourdes to London. It turned out that Rosario had been the cleaner in Casa Carolina for many years. I asked if she knew Antonio, the gardener; she knew him rather well, actually: he was her father. It was also a delight to be able to so easily understand Javier's unaccented Spanish. Born and brought up in Barcelona, though married to a village girl, to me he sounded like a newsreader. With hospitality typical of Andalucíans, they enquired whether we would join them at their house for dinner the following week. Over time they have become our best friends in the village, and we are now proud godparents to Claudia and her little brother, Nicolas, one of the three bumps at Lourdes's party.

Life was as perfect as it is allowed to be. There is a Southern Spanish expression, originating from the time of Arab occupation, that 'only God is perfect'. That perfection was marred one Saturday morning when Lourdes arrived to prepare Casa Rosa for clients, when the house had been empty for a week. Although she was trying to hide her distress, her face is always a mirror of her emotions. She told me to stay where I was and asked Stephen to follow her next door. Of course, that was a red rag to a bull; I was right behind them. Curled up, seemingly asleep in the sun between the roses and the lavender, was Picasso, but even the Mediterranean sun could not warm his lifeless body. He had always brought us little presents, baby birds occasionally, but more often mice and small rats. At the end of harvest each year, a lot of poison is spread to kill the rats that come out of the fields in this agricultural area. Picasso had caught his last rat. I cried all day, and the dogs, sensing our sadness, didn't leave our sides.

40

Fiesta Fiesta

Tradition dictates that the end of a building project is marked by a fiesta. Finishing work on Casa Carolina heralded our third. The catering, as always, was easy: plates of hams and cheeses, huge salads and about 40 sticks of bread. The cooking on these occasions is men's work, kid stew cooked in an industrial-sized pan, with a sauce of ground almonds, pine nuts, onions, garlic and the local wine, simmered over an open fire.

The only thing that differed this time was that when, as usual, we offered to provide the meat ready for cooking, Paco accepted our offer. It was, we thought, a sign that finally, after years, we were being trusted with such an important task. We arranged with Lourdes that Julio would have two of the poor little things ready for Stephen to pick up when he took her back to the village the following day. They were skinned and hanging in her shed. About four months old, they were roughly the same size as Niña.

'Lourdes, they need carving up.'

'Yes, tell Jackie that first she must . . . ah, Jackie.'

'If I go home with these, like this, I will be as dead as they are.'

'Yes, I was forgetting, but I think you are right.'

They spent an hour and a half on her kitchen floor butchering the kids. Stephen came back looking slightly pale and carrying two big bin liners, which he tried to 'hide' in the fridge. That evening, Paco and Antonio Bigote arrived early to start the cooking. At our previous two fiestas, we had eaten the M&S food-hall version of kid stew. It always arrived pre-cooked and just needed to be heated on the barbecue. This time, we were starting from scratch.

Sitting on the steps of the terrace, Bigote had both hands, obviously working away, inside one of the black bags.

'Antonio, what are you doing?'

'Jackie, you don't want to know.'

'I do, Antonio.'

'Jackie, you don't want to know.'

'I do, Antonio.'

'I am cutting the tongues and eyes out of the heads.'

'You were right, Antonio, I didn't want to know that.'

People arrived: actually, men arrived – this is a builders' fiesta. As the woman of the house I was there, of course, and, in fact, my eighty-year-old mother and her lifelong friend, Brenda, a mere spring chicken of seventy-seven, were here on holiday, but it was not in general a 'bring-your-loved-one' sort of occasion. Years later at our next fiesta, we turned this idea on its head with hilarious results.

Paco, as head builder, had now assumed the role of head chef.

'Jackie, I put a jug in your fridge when I arrived. Could you get it for me?'

'Here, Paco. What is it?'

'Jackie, you don't want to know.'

'I do, Paco.'

'Jackie, you don't want to know.'

'I do, Paco.'

'OK. It's the blood that was drained from the animals when their throats were cut; it makes the sauce rich and thick.'

'You were right, Paco, I didn't want to know that.'

He smiled. We ate at midnight, the goat stew was pronounced excellent, and when I found Paco and Bigote huddled in a corner looking secretive, I should have known better.

'What are you two doing?'

'Jackie, you don't want to know.'

'I do.'

'Jackie, you don't want to know.'

'I do.'

'We are eating the brains, they are the best bits.'

They were right, of course: I really didn't want to know. It was a great night, hot and still; the cicadas joined the party, competing with the men to see who could make more noise. The perfume from the honeysuckle and summer jasmine was at its peak, and there was a full moon reflected in the swimming pool. Mum and Brenda proved themselves impressively good at the rumba and passable at a paso doble.

Paco's younger brother – if you think Antonio Banderas is cute, then you would seriously fall for José Antonio – is the local policeman and was on duty that night. At about two in the morning, he arrived in uniform driving the jeep with 'POLICÍA LOCAL' in huge letters on the side. He parked it on the steep track at the side of our house and jumped over the wall to avoid being seen. The 'one beer' turned into more than several, and four hours later he left as he had arrived, over the wall, saying that he would let the car roll back down the hill and then turn the lights on when he reached the road so as not to attract attention. Two minutes later he rolled the jeep down the track, but instead of flicking the switch for the headlights, he hit the siren by mistake and woke the whole village.

41

Claudia

Walking back from a long, lazy lunch in the church square with my aunt, uncle, Javier, Rosario and their children, Claudia and her little brother, Nicolas, we came upon three old women all dressed in their black widow's weeds, tutting and peering at a bundle in the long grass.

It was the opening scene from *Macbeth* without the cauldron. Here, traditionally, the women wear black for three years after their mothers die, five years in black are deemed appropriate for the loss of a father, and for ever after, if and, usually, when, they become widows. It was just before the Easter celebrations, and all three had obviously treated themselves to a visit to the hairdresser. The older women, whose naturally jet-black hair goes almost pure white with age, favour an enhancing tint that, caught in the right light, gives their heads a slightly eerie faint-purple sheen.

One of these women was in tears. The bundle in the grass was her cat, no more than two years old, with teats full of milk and very near to death. Poison is a problem in this agricultural area, where it is used with the usual Spanish abandon. Therefore a cat that is 'a mouser' can be unlucky if its catch has already taken the bait. As you know, we lost our Picasso the same way.

She fumbled in her apron, and I thought she was looking for a handkerchief. What she produced was far smaller: the only surviving kitten. The mother was a beautiful tabby, exactly the type I have always so admired, but she must have had a night of wild passion with a ginger tom, and Auntie Margaret and I found ourselves peering down at one of the results.

Of course, the old lady saw us coming. By now we were very well known to the village people, and, I am sure, we had the reputation for being soft with animals. I know we should have just walked on; in fact, Stephen, Uncle Richard, Javier and Rosario had done just that. When Margaret and I caught up with them a few minutes later, there wasn't even a flicker of surprise on Stephen's face when my right boob began to take on a life of its own. I have always tucked the little ones down the front of my tops: it seems to settle them, though it has the opposite effect on Stephen. Claudia, now five and a half, was delighted with the new addition, and in a fit of emotion, I named the tiny kitten after her. Stephen looked towards the heavens, rolled his eyes and pointed out in a harsh, hissy whisper that there was a strong possibility that it wouldn't survive, and how was I going to explain that to her namesake. Me and my big mouth: he was right, as usual.

But survive she did. Much as I love animals, I have always believed that their place in life is second, if only a very minor second, to most humans. So why was I heating milk for her bottle at six in the morning, and still in my dressing gown at ten, after the next feed? Why was I talking to friends on the phone – there was no way I could leave the house – about the fact that she was now sleeping for five hours through the night? I smelled of formula milk – my clothes were covered in it – and she often peed all over me. She slept in a shoebox on my bedside table, wrapped in a pale baby-blue cashmere pashmina. Our vet advised that the four-hourly feeds we had last seen with Domingo were, this time, even more important.

'She is too small to know when she is hungry. Unlike a human baby, she will not cry, she will just sleep until . . .'

Rafael frightened the life out of me; I surrounded her shoebox with three alarm clocks.

Within a week, she began to move around, quickly working out how her front legs worked but couldn't master the back; she kept going round in circles. But it wasn't long before she could cross the terrace faster than us, though she was still a baby. She loved being swaddled in her blanket and sucking at her bottle so hard that her little ears waggled with the effort.

Domingo fell in love with her. He followed her everywhere, growling at the others when they got too close; he even bared his teeth at Charly. He washed her face after meals and her bottom after – I'm sure you get the idea.

42

Bamboleo

The day of Carmen, the fisherman's saint, is 16 July. As the sun
dips, her statues are taken from churches to the beaches all along
the coast. They are then put onto fishing boats for a trip to sea
to pray for the safety of her men and for good catches in the
coming year. The older local people wouldn't dream of swimming
in the sea before this day of blessing, despite temperatures in the
eighties. They wait, each year, until the sea has been blessed and
therefore cleansed. Every available craft follows Carmen in this
procession; the fishing fleet from each port is scrubbed clean, their
rigging covered in flags and bunting, their horns tooting. Each
boat carries about a hundred family and friends. At the other end
of the scale are the tiny inflatables with outboard motors carrying
two or three brave teenagers, bobbing around alarmingly in the
wake of the larger boats.

We were invited by neighbours to join them on their small
sailing boat, moored at Caleta, for the evening of Carmen, and
we eagerly accepted. Caleta de Vélez does not make its living as
a harbour for yachts. Marina del Este, half an hour's drive east
of Nerja, is the closest to a luxury harbour we have around here.
It has the required art gallery, designer-clothes shops and overpriced restaurants, whereas Caleta is very much a working port
about 20 minutes' drive back along the coast towards Málaga.
At six every morning, except for Mondays, the fish are auctioned

by the crateload. We have only managed to get there for the auction once in all our time here (I don't really 'do' 6 a.m. any more), but it was memorable. Some of the last boats to come back were still circling just outside the harbour walls, sorting their catches and throwing guts overboard to the delight of the swarming, squawking seagulls.

Inside the cavernous shed that is the market, men still in oilskins stood over their catches doing their deals with suited businessmen wearing wellingtons and wielding calculators and mobile phones. The contrast in cultures was striking. Most of the contents of most of the crates were still squirming; several crabs were halfway across the floor with an obviously pre-planned escape route; the smell was pungent. Large articulated refrigerated lorries sat by the dock with their engines running, waiting for the deals to be done and to be on their way to Málaga, Sevilla and even Madrid. The Spanish people pride themselves on the freshness of their fish. Lourdes wouldn't dream of buying a clam unless it was still sticking its tongue out at her.

On the night of Carmen, we arrived at the port at seven and lurched on board, greeted our fellow guests and set off back towards Nerja. The journey that had just taken us twenty minutes in the car was reversed on water and took over two hours. To begin with, the sails were up in an optimistic yet futile attempt to catch the few puffs of warm air that could not even be called a breeze. While the sails were up, flexibility was essential. Booms, or whatever you call the things that swing the sails around, were booming. Years of yoga are to be recommended when you are suddenly commanded to raise your feet, duck your head and twist to the right.

Admitting defeat, the outboard engine was coaxed to life, and we chugged along very enjoyably with a beer in hand, the sun setting, and a most welcome respite from the landlocked heat of the day. For us, it was the first chance to see from sea the coastline that we knew so well, giving it a completely different perspective.

We arrived off the Balcón at nine. The Balcón de Europa is a local landmark: a rocky promontory jutting out to sea and approached, landside, by a wide avenue of 80-foot palm trees, it is the social centre of the town. It is the place where every Sunday evening the town's people dress in their finest and take the air. The children are scrubbed and polished, the girls with the satin bows in their hair matching those on the backs of their smocked dresses. Little boys wear junior suits with ties and waistcoats, and you have to hunt to find the small babies amongst the lacy frills of their prams. It is also the place where the tourists photograph each other, eat ice cream and pay too much for a coffee, and, these days, where many street performers ply their trades. You can have your portrait painted, your cards read, your hair beaded and braided. You can listen to the South American group playing pan pipes or just stand watching the beautiful young couple who dance superb tango.

That night, however, we were in the privileged position of looking up at the packed crowds on the Balcón from our space on the sea. Carmen was delivered to the shore on the men's shoulders, was reverently installed in the honoured boat and set off on her annual tour of the coast. As the light faded, a tiny motorboat hired by the town hall did its rounds, throwing flares into the sea and handing out long tapers to all the 'boat people'. By this torchlight, to shouts of 'Viva, Viva, Carmen, Guapa Viva' ('Long live Carmen, our beautiful Carmen'), we arrived back in front of the Balcón for the firework display. We had heard several people rave about how good the firework display was at the festival for Carmen. Our host reversed the boat a little further away from the shore and scooped up two big buckets of seawater to have at hand just in case. We sat watching with anticipation. What appeared to be a small rocket was fired from the little beach below the Balcón: trailing a feeble phosphorus glow, it arced 50 feet into the air and then plopped into the sea. I turned to Stephen and raised an eyebrow; less than impressed, he shrugged. After a slow count of ten, the sea in front of us exploded with lurid sparks, colour and noise. Water fireworks – I had never seen them before – they were indeed spectacular.

It was a memorable evening and certainly fuelled Stephen's enthusiasm for buying a boat – even I was coming round to the idea – then we set off for home. Still no wind and so once again the tiny motor was asked to do its best. It was suddenly cold. A cotton jumper I had with me 'just in case' had proved essential but far from enough. We were going against the swell and sitting on duckboard benches that my backside hadn't experienced since school changing-rooms over 30 years before. The return journey took three and a half hours.

'Jackie, how about a trip to Málaga tomorrow?'

'No, there's nothing we really need.'

'There are two or three boat showrooms.'

He ducked, I missed and the subject was dropped for a few days. But when he judged that the bruises on my bum had faded sufficiently, we went back to the subject of boats.

Although an architect by training, Stephen is also a very good salesman. Knowing that 'horsepower' sort of words would leave me cold, he painted a lifestyle picture of lazy days moored off the coast, away from the madding August crowds, diving into crystal-clear water and picnicking in isolated coves. When I started joining in the discussion of what sort of boat we might buy, we both knew it was only a matter of time. I was insistent that it had to be something that would not take us over three hours to travel the distance that a car could do in twenty minutes. Duckboard seats were out of the question, and it had to have a toilet. (It's a girl thing.) My final plea, trying to relate to his technical side, was that it had to be *vroom vroom* not *chug chug*.

We bought a boat. It's a Rinker . . . ? (Ask Stephen, I don't have a clue.) It is basically a floating bar, and on the rare occasions that we use it, it is great fun. It has padded leather seats, a loo, and does *vroom vroom* very nicely. To register a boat, it has to

have a name, and we wanted to call it something Spanish. We
went through all our music CDs looking for inspiration and
settled on an old Gipsy Kings song, 'Bamboleo', meaning 'to
sway rhythmically'.

43

Back to the Plot

By the plot, I mean the piece of land, here called a *parcela*, that we acquired when we bought Casa Carolina. We were always going to build on it one day, but during our first few years of retirement we had moved into La Panificadora and changed most of the floors, gutted the kitchen and landscaped the gardens. We had put pools into Casas Rosa and Carolina, and built Carmen in Maro up from its ruins. I was begging for the summer off, and much as I liked Paco and his team, I didn't want to see them again, other than socially, for a long, long time.

Stephen had other ideas; this was an architect's dream. Here was his chance to build from scratch, no restrictions apart from the fact that the site was full of mature trees. How could he weave his design to save as many as possible? We had seven tall pines full of cones, six proud green-black cypresses thirty feet high and at least a dozen mimosa that each spring paraded their yellow fluff like Easter chicks.

Back to the 'paper-tablecloth' school of design. This was to be our fourth house to go on the rental market. Over long lunches, we designed La Quinta. When I say 'we' designed, what I mean is that Stephen designed a beautiful house and when I came up with often charming, but usually fanciful and totally impractical, ideas, he would turn them into a workable reality. Together we got it right.

I did actually get most of that summer off. The architectural drawing package that Stephen bought for the computer kept him out of trouble for weeks before he even produced a working drawing. Then came the process of obtaining quotes, planning permissions and appointing contractors. Meanwhile, we went back to the fun bit: scouring the old building sites, junkyards and skips, finding, for example, a front door of old olive wood with a little iron-crossed window. It looked like nothing when we bought it for very little, but after a drink of turpentine and several coats of linseed oil, it was magnificent.

Much like the UK in the '50s and '60s, most Spanish people are now embracing anything and everything modern. Wooden doors and windows are being replaced by aluminium double glazing, stone sinks are put out with the rubbish and the traditional crafts are being lost and forgotten. Skips outside of old houses are now our treasure troves, though it is still possible to persuade many of the local potters and ironmongers to produce their old work. On first meeting, they proudly show how far they have moved with the times, producing examples of hideous tiles or gates. When we explain what we are looking for, they seem bemused and often slightly disappointed; however, without exception, they are always delighted with the end result. Manolo, the iron man, told us that he took the gates we asked him to make from Stephen's drawings to show his 80-year-old father, from whom he had learned his trade. It made his week.

We had been impressed by José, who had built the shells for the pools in both Carmen and Carolina. Since then, he had grown his offer to include the concrete structures for houses, essential here because it is deemed to be an earthquake zone. Although the last recorded tremor to do any damage was in 1899, we often read in the local papers that there had been enough of a wobble to register, the most recent only a month ago. So José got the job of structure; after that, the builders would move in.

'Which building team are you going to use?'

'Paco's.'

'Every time you do, you swear it will be the last.'

'And I'm sure this will be no exception.'

It wasn't.

In the spring of the year 2000, the digger arrived to excavate the foundations that had been marked out by walking the site trailing handfuls of sand to define the lines. The skill of the operator was impressive, using the scoop with the ease of a giant third hand to gouge out the earth. Paco was standing with us watching the first ground-breaking; he always seems to be around for the exciting moments, but never for the day-to-day grind that is always part of the building process.

'By the way, Paco, I tried to get you on your mobile number yesterday but got nothing; has the number changed?'

'I got rid of it. People kept calling me.'

Four open-bed lorries were shuttling the excavated earth away. It was very poor-quality soil, not worth keeping. About two feet down, the machine began to come up with huge rocks and boulders. Paco began muttering about the extra cost of removing them; they would have to go to a different place by a different lorry. They stayed, and now form the most beautiful rock gardens. Visiting friends tell us that after the craze for garden-improvement programmes on British television, rocks that we would have had to pay to be removed are now selling for a fortune.

Two habits were established during the building of La Quinta. First, almost every evening, we would take a bottle of wine and walk the site at around six thirty, just after the builders had left. Every day there was progress, from bare concrete columns to bricks beginning to form walls. We nearly came to blows at this stage because I couldn't believe that some of the rooms were going to be big enough to even swing a cat, but Stephen was confident and used to the false illusions that appear at this stage of building. As it has turned out, you could easily swing two cats in even the smallest rooms, something I have never actually tried, but have often been sorely tempted.

The roof went on. Two concrete ramps that would eventually become the staircase to the upper floor meant that for the first time I saw the spectacular views down to the sea and up to the mountains from that level. I hate heights (standing on a chair is a huge act of bravery for me) and therefore I had never been persuaded, despite much hand-clapping and shouts of 'go, go, go' from our builders, to climb the ladder and balance on a concrete girder. Until this stage, I had had to content myself with listening to Stephen waxing lyrical. Every day there were decisions to be taken, but to watch a house grow from a drawing, changing from two dimensions to three, was both an education and a delight.

Our second habit was generated by Ron and Anne, an English couple who had lived here for many years and were only five minutes' walk away from La Quinta. Stephen met Ron through golf, and I was subsequently introduced to Anne at a restaurant in the mountains above the village. A classic example of the attraction of opposites, we all got on famously. Ron was a big loud bear of a man, always the life and soul of the party, telling jokes and buying rounds. Beneath this brash exterior was one of the warmest souls I have ever been lucky enough to meet. He was an OK golfer and a very, very talented squash and tennis player, with a penchant for loud silk shirts and prawns pil-pil. 'Larger than life' was a good description of Ron, and I hope that is true, because he is no longer with us.

The builders finished at three on Friday afternoons, having worked through their lunch hour. Almost every Friday, Ron and Anne would arrive with a chilled bottle of wine and smoked-salmon sandwiches. Both of them had a fondness for white trousers and shoes, but the place was filthy; we never knew where to suggest they sat. They were friends of the calibre that stuck to their high standards of dress but still visited us anyway. Over time, we progressed from perching our bums on breeze blocks in the garden to sitting on the covered terrace and, finally, eating our lunch on the newly installed granite slab that was the terrace table. Every week, as Ron watched the house grow, he became more and more insistent that we should move into it. It became a joke between us. Ron would argue, quite rightly, that there would be much more space for our four dogs, and for the ones that we were bound to acquire in the future. I would counter that we were never going to have more than four dogs, and anyway, we had not designed the house for us. My home and heart were now settled in La Molineta: La Panificadora was my home. Having spent a nomadic life, I was never going to move again.

44

Three Little Shits

By the following March, Stephen, Lourdes and I were painting the new house. The builders had finished most of the interior and were laying the terracotta terrace tiles and building planters around the pool. It takes a lot of hours and hard work to paint a house from scratch: the newly plastered walls drink up the first two coats in a most depressing way. A room will look good when you finish of an evening, yet by morning the walls once again seem grey. Bare-wood doors and window frames behave in the same way. We spent a small fortune on paint, brushes and white spirit in the village *ferretería* (ironmongers), and have the free baseball caps, T-shirts and pens all carrying their logo – 'Pinturas Andalucía' – to prove it. To get the cement off the tiles requires *agua fuerte*, literally 'strong water'. This is a bit of an understatement: *agua fuerte* is hydrochloric acid, and as you pour it on the tiles, the excess cement turns green, bubbles and froths. As we worked backwards across the floors, no matter how careful we were our legs came up in blisters.

The plot had always been enclosed by three-foot-high dry-stone walls and wrought-iron gates. One morning, Stephen dropped me at the house on his way up to the village for yet more paint. Remembering that we also needed gloss and masking tape, I ran back to the gate.

'Stephen, wait, we need more . . . Oh shit . . . Oh shit . . . *Oh shit.*'

By the gate, inside our enclosed land, was the pile of empty wooden pallets that the bricks and tiles had arrived on. From behind these appeared a tiny jet-black puppy, swiftly followed by another, motley black-and-brown, and then yet another, again jet-black but with classic border-collie white markings of face, socks and tail. They stood there, their baby-blue eyes wide and staring, huddled together and trembling.

'Stephen, I think you had better come here.'

'Darling, are you all right?'

'I'm fine – well I was – but look.'

'Oh shit.'

'How did they get here?'

'How do you think? Someone has dropped them over the wall; they didn't parachute in, did they? It's probably someone who knows just how daft we are. Not this time, though, we can't have any more dogs.'

'I agree.'

Plans to paint were forgotten. Stephen went home with instructions to return with milk and food. Charly, Domingo, Niña and Tintin had long been weaned onto a diet of dry biscuits and kitchen scraps, with bones as treats, but these little bundles were far too small to manage hard food. Stephen returned with two packets of *jamón* Serrano and a carton of milk. They were starving. The all-black puppy was the boldest of the three and was soon wolfing the ham from my hand while I called him a little pig. The other two hesitantly followed his lead. After a breakfast fit for kings, they were much more relaxed and friendly, and I checked out their 'bits', establishing that we had two boys and a girl. The girl, black with white, was the image of the sheepdog puppies in one of my all-time favourite smilie movies about a pig called Babe. Exhausted by their plight and with full, bald little pink bellies, they cuddled up together into a corner of the bare dusty floor and were soon fast asleep, one breathing bundle of fur: it was impossible to define where one started and another stopped.

We sat watching the sleeping puppies. I think we were slightly stunned. The four dogs we had were with us as the results of decisions to take on another dog. These three had literally been dumped upon us.

'Right. Who do we know that wants a dog?'

'Jackie, nobody around here wants a dog. If you want a dog, there are hundreds around here. You know that; why do you think these have been abandoned?'

'OK. Who do we know that doesn't yet know that they want a dog?'

I had been in marketing for 20 years. While I was busy trying to think of potential homes for the puppies, Stephen was busy trying to work out who might have left them here in the first place and return them promptly.

Almost our first tenants in Casa Rosa were Lynn and Tony, a couple from Devon that we grew to like very much. They went on to spend many holidays in our little house in Maro and, like us, they fell in love with Spain. On their retirement, they moved out here with their three springer spaniels, settling in a peaceful spot close to Lake Viñuela. We met regularly for lunch.

'How about Lynn and Tony?'

'They already have three.'

'Well, as of this morning, we have *seven*; it's worth a try.'

Life-long dog lovers, they eagerly agreed to come and have a look at the new arrivals, but only on the understanding that there was no way that they were in the market for a puppy.

We all sat on the newly constructed terrace, amidst the builders' rubble, watching the three of them at play. After their initial nap, the puppies had woken full of the joys of life, eager for more food and ready to explore. I am always amazed at how resilient young animals are, but as a trio, they were formidable. The fact that they had been abandoned and, I assume, snatched from their mother seemed to have been forgotten. Stephen popped home for supplies for us all, returning with tins of tuna (we were out of ham by then) and bottles of wine. It was a lovely afternoon, only tempered by the problem of what to do with the puppies.

The brindle-coloured boy had taken to Tony and Lynn in a big way, and the affection was obviously mutual. I had already started to call him Stumpy, his tail being far shorter than those of his siblings. Despite my best salesman's patter all afternoon, Lynn and Tony were about to leave and we still had the three pups. I had talked about the new lease of life a puppy would give to their much older springers, about the fact that, being so young, a new puppy would be no threat to the existing pack. I even used the emotional blackmail of telling Stephen that we would have to consider having them put down if we couldn't find homes for them. Four hours and three bottles of wine later, it hadn't worked. Tony remembered he had something for us in his car and went to get it while Lynn packed up their things. He returned carrying a deep cardboard box, inside which was an old blanket. He had a big grin on his face.

'We knew the moment you called that we wouldn't be able to resist, but it's been fun watching you two try so hard all afternoon.'

I didn't know whether to hit him or kiss him, so I did both. They chose Stumpy and, quite rightly, immediately renamed him Pablo. Almost certainly born in Málaga Province, like the artist before him.

One down, two to go: not bad for the first few hours. We took the little pig and his sister home for the night. Charly, who four years before had thoroughly enjoyed his status as an only child, rolled his eyes in disgust and chuffed. Niña and Tintin feigned indifference. Domingo, on the other hand, made them very welcome; suddenly, he was the fourth-tallest dog in the house and seemed to relish his new status.

That Sunday we had an invitation to a birthday party, and until this point we had been wondering whether or not to go and how to make our excuses. It would be full of expats and not really our sort of thing, but now it would be a great hunting ground for homes for the puppies. Much to their disgust, we gave them a bath; they fluffed up beautifully and smelled delicious. Carrying one each, we arrived and everyone fell in love with them. They were passed around like cuddly toys, and I followed, explaining their story and pointing out that they were free to good homes. We lost them for most of the afternoon; this was looking promising. But sadly we left the party as we arrived, carrying one each.

The following Friday, Ron could hardly contain his delight. As usual, we were sitting on the terrace with our smoked-salmon sandwiches and glasses of wine. This time, though, we had puppies playing at our feet. They were still so tiny that we didn't want to risk leaving them alone all day with the older dogs, who, with the exception of Domingo, to a man (sorry Niña), were less than impressed by their arrival, and therefore we had been bringing them with us every day.

'Face it, Jackie, you two will have to move here now.'

'Why, Ron?'

'Six dogs.'

'No. We have four dogs; we will find homes for these puppies.'

In my heart I knew that this was probably not true, and in the ten days that we had had them, I was so touched by the way they behaved with each other. It was the first time I had seen puppies of about six weeks still together. They needed less attention than a pup of that age on its own, they explored their new world with such eager enthusiasm and then, when frightened, tired or hungry, ran to each other for comfort. They slept with their arms around each other and, in an act of 'penis envy', Babe spent most of her days play-fighting, puppy-bowing and trying to chew Piglet's willy off. Piglet: more polite than calling him a little pig, which he was, and Babe as in the movie, his pretty little sister. They ran around the building site as if joined at the hip, Piglet's pure-black tail and Babe's with a white tip, fanning through the air like plumes on the helmets of medieval knights.

'We couldn't possibly split them up now. We will have to find someone who will take them both.'

'We can't find anyone who will take *one*.'

'But Stephen, just look at them together.'

'We don't need more dogs.'

'I know that. Cute, aren't they?'

'We don't need more dogs.'

'I know. Aren't they just the most adorable things you have ever seen?'

That evening, Stephen worked until the early hours redesigning parts of La Quinta to overcome my objections and explanations as to why we could not possibly move there. It had been designed and built for people on holiday. It had also been designed and built with a lot of love and care; we chose tiles, furniture and fittings that we would have wanted for ourselves, but there is a difference between a house for holidays and a permanent home. For a start, much less storage, smaller wardrobes, less kitchen space. Overnight he created, on paper, a pantry off the kitchen and a dressing-room off the master bedroom. Now they are two of my favourite rooms. We agreed to turn the third bedroom into our study and build a guest cottage at the bottom of the garden. It meant an extra month's work for Paco's team and knocking holes in a few already painted walls, but on 4 July we moved in with our *six* dogs.

45

Lourdes the Landlady

Over the last four years, Lourdes has become much more sophisticated. Of course, all things are relative, but money in her pocket has definitely altered her views, and there are friends of ours who accuse us of having corrupted her. However, it is a time of change around here: we may, in her case, have been the catalyst, but the change was inevitable.

For many years, her family has had a small *cortijo* in the foothills of the mountains, about two miles above the village. There are many such buildings around here, almost identical to ours. They are seemingly scattered at random; from a distance, it looks as if God has thrown handfuls of white pebbles at the mountainside. Originally they were used for storing the tools to work the fields and to take siestas away from the blistering heat of an Andalucían summer afternoon. As time went on, another room would be added, then cooking facilities. These places had no electricity and only cold water from a well – as, indeed, ours still has – but nowadays many have a living room, kitchen, bathroom and one or two bedrooms. It is common in summer for families lucky enough to have such a place to leave the village at the weekends and spend a couple of nights enjoying the cooler air coming down from the mountains.

Julio used their *cortijo* for its traditional purpose: it is no more than 300 yards from the corral, home to his 300 goats. In summer, the smells and the flies are really quite impressive. One summer, Lourdes started asking me about renting out houses for holidays. Having just moved into La Quinta, we now had four houses on the rental market and a veritable army of gardeners and cleaners. We had visited Lourdes's *cortijo* many times. It was difficult to find a diplomatic way to tell her that I didn't think it would qualify as most holidaymakers' idea of a Spanish villa, though it was, of course, immaculately clean. An old water-storage tank had been lined with an odd assortment of tiles and made a perfectly serviceable pool, and the views were fantastic, but it was, and would always be, 300 yards from 300 goats and very, very basic.

I was amazed when, a short time later, Lourdes reported that through a Spanish agent she had signed a rental contract with an English tour operator and that her first clients would arrive at the end of that month. I was amazed; Julio was furious. He was losing his bolt-hole, and anyway, with them both working, they had, as far as he could see, more than enough money for the three of them; there was no need for it.

The first, and last, people to rent the place arrived on a Saturday afternoon. Julio, as usual, was out with his herd. We have often passed him many miles from home, squatting on the side of a mountain, an olive tree for shade, casually throwing stones just in front of straying goats with the accuracy of a professional darts player. That day, returning less than impressed to see a rental car parked outside and foreigners sitting on his terrace, he decided to change the site of his Saturday-evening ritual.

Kid is a delicacy around here, and Sunday lunch when family are visiting demands it. So every Saturday night he butchers to order. That evening, the order was for three. In full view of the new arrivals, he took three baby goats into the side yard of the corral, slit their throats and hung them up to bleed.

The clients left the following day, still hysterical. It was the last booking that Lourdes ever had.

46

Marbella

Lourdes was not the only local person to be disappointed that summer: with a demand for holiday accommodation that far outstripped supply, the previous winter all the tour operators had greedily signed up anything and everything, but most had problems of one sort or another. A common complaint was access roads: people would arrive late at night, driving a strange car on the wrong side of the road, and have to negotiate tracks to reach their houses that would make a mountaineer blanch, and if it rained while they were out, they often couldn't get back.

By way of compensation for their lack of promised income, the tour operators combined forces to offer the disgruntled owners a free weekend in Marbella. Lourdes was delighted; it would be her second trip away from the village. Julio refused to go. There was a stand-off for a few days, and then she casually mentioned a programme she had been watching on television about stress and depression. One of the biggest causes of depression, she pointed out, was not getting out enough. It was something very expensive to treat, sufferers couldn't work; she hoped she wouldn't get it, but it was always possible. It was agreed that they would go to Marbella for one night on the condition that they leave at six the following morning to be back in time for the goats' first milking. It would be Julio's first night out of his village in his 36 years and Lourdes's fourth.

I wish Lourdes could tell you this story herself. When she first told us, we were both aching with laughter. They arrived at the hotel in Marbella in Julio's *campo* van, several years old, normally used to transport animals and far too big to ever have seen a car wash. The back doors have been held together with a piece of rope for years, the exhaust pipe and the winder for the passenger window are long gone, the window is stuck in open mode, twigs and straw sprout from the two remaining hubcaps, and it stinks. Not thinking to borrow a suitcase, she packed their overnight things in two supermarket carrier bags. That is how they arrived in Marbella, holiday home to the rich, famous and villainous. Marbella, where *Hello!* magazine shoots so many of its doomed 'happy-couple' spreads.

In reception, she took over from Julio, having had experience of such things. They were given a room on the eighth floor, and Lourdes headed for the lift.

'What are you doing?'

'Waiting for the lift.'

'I don't trust them. Anyway, it's only eight floors. We will walk.'

Outside their room, Julio asked Lourdes for the key. She didn't have it. She walked back down eight flights of stairs to be told that her husband had been given a card, which was the key. She walked back up the eight floors, knowing that he was not going to be happy about this.

'You have the key, it is a card.'

'A card. You mean this?'

'I suppose so. The girl at reception says if you put it into the door, it will open.'

'Here the doors open with pieces of plastic? Was it the same in London, no keys?'

'No, in London we had keys.'

It took them ten minutes to get the door open, never waiting for the green light before trying the handle. I won't bother you with the details, but the room's electricity was also operated on the same principle and they spent their first hour in semi-darkness until Lourdes once more walked down to reception for an explanation (and cheated by catching the lift on the way back). Julio, meanwhile, propped a chair under the handle and wedged a shoe under the door, muttering about not trusting doors without keys, especially in a foreign village.

That afternoon, there was a free coach trip to one of Spain's biggest department stores, El Corte Inglés in Puerto Banús. I had taken Lourdes to the sister store in Málaga the year before and she had loved it.

'Julio, we must go, and it's free.'

'Why? There are plenty of shops in the village. You are always in the shops.'

'But Julio, this is different, it is all the shops in the village and many, many more, all in one place, they have everything.'

'Everything? Then we will go.'

It is true that there are now many shops in the village. The ones selling guidebooks, postcards and gaudy ceramics leap out at you from the pavements, whereas the butchers, bakers and general grocers are mainly hidden behind doors covered by woven curtains and have to be discovered. Inside are three or four chairs, and the shoppers are in a hurry if they spend less than an hour buying two eggs and a slice of ham, and the provisions for the day take second place to the gossip from the day before. Rather different to El Corte Inglés, which could be likened to Selfridges.

'Where first, Julio?'

"Well, I would like to see the goat department.'

She was caught. Having claimed the store had everything, she could not satisfy Julio with a visit to the pet shop. He sulked for the rest of the afternoon and refused to be impressed at her mastery of the escalators (he used the stairs).

When they had first arrived and eventually got into their room, the free bingo tickets for that evening's game in the hotel were sitting on the dressing table, yet another bonus for Lourdes. She was used to the bingo played at *feria*. Standing in front of loud stalls laden with their cheap stereos and enormous stuffed-toy prizes, she would then tear her losing tickets into pieces with disdain and, like her fellow players, scatter them on the floor, making the surrounding area look like a good tapas bar in the late afternoon.

That evening's prizes were cash, and the top prize was more than a month's wages for Lourdes. She was almost totally focused, but glanced round for a second to find Julio staring out of the window, his card in his lap.

'Julio, you must pay attention.'

'I have been paying attention. I got all the numbers more than two minutes ago, this game is really boring.'

Lourdes grabbed his card and, as she did so, someone on the other side of the room shouted 'bingo'. She ran to the caller, explained that her husband had never played the game before and yet his numbers had come up first, but, of course, to no avail. The following morning, with a heavy silence between them, they left before five to get back to the goats. That was Julio's first and, I somehow suspect, his last night away from his village.

47

The Great Escape

As I have said, everyone who tries to pin a breed to Tintin comes up with lurcher. Even after almost three years with us, he still weighs next to nothing, and although he is the tallest of them all, I can pick him up with ease. Walking with the dogs in the mountains, when T.T.'s long legs are at full stride he doubles the pace of the others and frequently jumps over their heads to get where he's going. This agility includes the vertical; he is a four-legged pogo stick.

The dry-stone walls that surround La Quinta were about three feet high before we moved in. With Tintin in mind, we built them up to five feet – and still he escaped. He is now a social animal, making up for lost time. Having been terrified of people for the first year of his life, he now believes they can do no wrong and wants to meet as many as possible. The problem with this is that he has no road sense: not only is he a danger to himself but also to drivers, so we commissioned Manolo, our iron man, to make railings to run along the top of the wall. Meanwhile, during the day, we tethered Tintin by his lead to a long length of wire pegged firmly into the ground at both ends; it allowed him to move around and seek sun or shade, but not to escape. At night, we shut all the dogs in the house, against our usual practice of leaving terrace doors open and letting them come and go at will. It was far from ideal, but was the best we

could do. Manolo would take three weeks to make and install
the railings, and then Tintin would be free to run within the
garden and safe. Or so we thought. Friends called to say that
their neighbours were worried because they hadn't seen Tintin
for a few days. We had never met these people, but apparently,
during our first month in La Quinta, his month of freedom,
every evening T.T. would arrive at their house, half a mile from
us, to eat his first supper. They had a stock of dog food for him;
he ate, slept on their sofa or their bed for half an hour or so;
had a cuddle and then came home.

With the last section of railings in place, we paid Manolo's
bill, decided that Tintin must be the most expensive mutt in
Andalucía, and took a bottle of cava into the garden to celebrate
his liberty from both the wire and his captivity. The cork popped,
we undid his collar and, after a few seconds of confusion, he
realised that he was no longer restricted. He barked with
excitement, circled the very large garden several times and kept
returning to us with a waggy tail.

'Look at Charly: he was born old, he's definitely been here
before, I wonder who he was. This is perfect, now they are all
safe. The puppies are asleep in the grass and Domingo and
Niña are enjoying the sunshine. Umm, Stephen, when did you
last see Tintin?'

'About ten minutes ago, he was on the bottom wall in the
corner . . . Oh no, he can't have.'

He was gone again. As usual he came back within the hour,
yet it took us another month to finally make the garden secure.
We had to wire up junctions where the railings met at corners
until our skinny Houdini couldn't slip through. Welcome to
La Quinta, also known as Colditz: every day we check for
tunnels.

48

Es La Vida

'*Es la vida*' – 'that's life' – is usually heard here in relation to death. When told that anyone over 60 has died, that's the response: *es la vida*. Infant mortality was so high in the village that there are two ways to ask an older woman how many children she has or had, because there are almost always two answers: first, the number of children born, and second, the number that survived. Even now, babies are rarely baptised with ceremony before the end of their first year, when their chances of surviving are deemed probable.

A death in the family is a sorrow shared by the village. If you die here before about ten in the morning, you will probably be buried late the same day. The church bells ring the death call and the news spreads rapidly around the village. If it's later in the day, you stay overnight in your house, usually laid out on the dining table, and all the people of the village visit to pay their respects; whether friends or enemies in life, all come to say goodbye. The men have it easy: they stand outside smoking and chatting; the women sit by the body all night and comfort the bereaved. Neighbours in the surrounding houses leave every light they have burning throughout the night to ward off bad spirits.

Lourdes arrived early one evening to tell us that Paco's father had just died. To be honest, we had fancied an early night, but it was not to be. Paco was our builder, and although we had only been on nodding terms with his father, Francisco, that was enough. It was expected that we go to his house. Outside there were at least a hundred people standing around, mainly men, including Paco and his younger brother, the local policeman, José Antonio, greeting newcomers and accepting their condolences; inside it was all women.

I entered the house behind Lourdes, leaving Stephen in the street, and copied everything she did. The wooden shutters were closed against the late evening sun; the room was lit only by candles. Sitting around one side of the open coffin were the new widow, her daughter and two daughters-in-law. All were dressed in black and holding Bibles. We joined the queue to kiss the grieving women and then found a little space in the corner of the very cramped room. Some of the women bent to kiss Francisco's cheek; more simply touched his face or his hand with a lingering look. I find it hard to describe why, but it was not the morbid occasion that I had expected. There were tears, of course, but also smiles and occasionally laughter, especially when someone told the story of him getting so drunk while his wife was in labour with Paco that he took one look at the newborn baby and went around the village banging on friends' doors at three in the morning to tell everyone about the arrival of his newborn daughter. Of course, his father missing the obvious is something that Paco still has to live with more than 40 years later. After two hours of standing there in silence, Lourdes said it would be respectable for me to leave now. I was instructed to leave quietly without goodbyes: 'Goodbyes to the living are not for this night.' She said she must stay for at least another three hours; Francisco's wife was her mother's second cousin. Close family would be there till dawn and traditionally would not eat from hearing the sad news until after the funeral.

Francisco was buried at five the next evening following a Mass in the church; again, the whole village was there. The Spanish, in death as in life, like to be close together. Graveyards are multi-storey constructions: coffins are slid into spaces almost on top of one another and then, while the mourners look on, the space is bricked up. Later it is plastered and a glass front is added; behind the glass are artificial flowers, ornate crosses and normally a picture of the person, often a favourite possession, too. When the graves are of children, their baby photos and cuddly toys make a heart-wrenching sight.

November the first is El Día de los Muertos, the Day of the Dead. Bunches of flowers double in price as everyone buys them to take to the graves; candles are lit; and many people spend this day, all day, beside their lost ones.

49

Number Seven

When La Quinta was still a building site, we would often get a visit from a beautiful big black cat with huge, almost emerald, green eyes. He was flirtatious, friendly and sometimes demanded a share of our sandwiches. We enjoyed his company but didn't really give him much thought. Moving in with our brood of dogs and cats caused this animal to undergo a personality transplant. He had been quite happy to share his territory with humans in exchange for scraps, but other animals on his patch were a totally different matter.

Pavarotti embarked on World War III, but having lost his masculinity under the scalpel of Rafael several years before, he was at a distinct disadvantage. His opponent had a full working set of eggs and the attitude to match. Poor Pavarotti, he would limp back from his campaigns to literally lick his wounds and still has a big split in his right ear for his troubles. After one of these battles he seemed particularly depressed and under the weather, so we took him to see Rafael and Dolores, who, much to Pavarotti's disgust, took a blood sample for analysis.

During this time, Pavarotti's little sister was of absolutely no help to him. The day we moved into La Quinta, Pantoja took one look around our new house, then walked the half-mile back to La Panificadora that same night. She repeated this journey at least two dozen times, and we retraced these journeys to collect her before we finally got her to settle. 'Butter on the paws' may be dismissed as an old wives' tale, but it worked for us (or rather for her).

Two days later, Stephen was in town at the vet's to get the results of the blood test that, thankfully, gave Pavarotti the all-clear. Feline Aids is rife around here and we had been worried that Attila the Cat might have infected him.

'That's a cute little puppy, Rafael. Is he yours?'

'He is cute, isn't he, and very bright too, but sadly he is blind.'

Stephen did a double take. The cute little puppy bouncing around the surgery was, occasionally, bumping into things, but that's what puppies do. When called he came running, wagging his stumpy little tail.

Rafael told his story. An English couple had brought him in a month before; he was their puppy, about six weeks old, with a high fever and very close to death: he had distemper. Distemper kills 50 per cent of the adult dogs and 80 per cent of the puppies that it infects. Rafael and Dolores had spent long days and nights nursing him back to health and were delighted with their success. His stumpy tail had not been docked; it had been infected and, therefore, half of it had had to go. This little mite had really been through hell. It was only when he was recovering and strong enough to undergo a full examination that they checked for all the symptoms and side effects that distemper can cause. They then realised he had not quite escaped: his optic nerves had been severely damaged. He was blind. On learning this, his owners asked that he be put to sleep, a request that Rafael refused. They paid their bill and walked away from him.

'We would love to keep him, he's such a brave little dog, and I suppose that is what we will end up doing if we have to, but we live in a flat and are out all day, it's not really fair. Of course, what he really needs is space, people who understand dogs, and other dogs around him – ideally several dogs, then he can become part of their pack, and they will then teach him all the things that no human can.'

I wasn't there, of course, but Stephen has described how Rafael came out with this statement. A lot of words from a man of few, and then he just left them hanging there.

'Rafael, may I use your phone?'

When the telephone rang, I was in the middle of promising myself that not only would we never, ever have another dog, but that we would somehow get rid of all the ones that we already had. This is quite a regular occurrence, this time brought about by the loss of a brand-new, never-even-worn pair of shoes (pale-blue, soft, soft leather kitten-heel slingbacks) to the twins Babe and Piglet's still needle-sharp baby teeth.

'It's me, I'm at the vet's. You're not going to like this.'

'Pavarotti's got Aids?'

'No. Pavo's fine, his blood test was clear.'

'What then?'

'Rafael has a puppy here . . .'

'No, no, no. Not in a million years. No way, I don't care what you say . . .'

'It's blind.'

'Blind. Oh, Stephen. No. Oh no, we couldn't manage, what about the others? No.'

'Apparently, the others are exactly what he needs, a pack around him. Look, darling, nobody else is going to take him, are they? What do you think?'

Stephen told Rafael that we would take him for a few days on the understanding that we could return him if he didn't get on with the others — or if we simply just couldn't cope with his disability.

I shut the dogs in the garden and waited for them to arrive. Every dog we have taken in has, at first, been overawed by its new surroundings. We are used to that, and are used to helping them, but I couldn't begin to imagine what a blind puppy would make of it all.

Stephen carried him in. On the phone I hadn't asked for a description; if we took in dogs on the basis of their looks, we would have fewer than we do (sorry, Tintin). As it turned out, he was one of the most beautiful little things I have ever seen. While waiting for them, I had been wondering, and, to be honest, worrying, what his eyes would be like. Ironically, they were huge, limpid chocolate-brown pools flecked with amber. Looking at him from above, he was black and short-haired, but he had a caramel lining and matching, slightly raised blobs over each eye. His ears belonged to a spaniel, as did the feathers on his back legs. We let him wander around the kitchen for a few minutes, but knew from experience that keeping him apart from the others for too long was not the way to go. Charly and Domingo were let in first: the oldest and calmest of the lot, they had seen it all before. As usual, Charly chuffed and sniffed, and Domingo, after a brief look, went straight to his basket – nobody takes his basket from him and, as usual, he wanted that established on day one.

Next came Niña and Tintin. Niña, always the most jealous, growled softly, sat in a corner and sulked. Tintin, on his own planet as usual, wagged his long ratty excuse for a tail in welcome and took the opportunity of our distraction to eat the cat biscuits in the pantry. The puppies, the twins, were no problem. Still at the stage where life is one big adventure, they did the bottom-sniffing bit and then ran back outside to play.

I once heard an old great-aunt of mine explaining to my young cousin why dogs sniff each other's bottoms. He had been watching her two little shih-tzus greeting her friend's Yorkshire terrier, and to the embarrassment of all but my aunt, he had pointed it out and asked why they do that. This was her reply.

'Many, many years ago, well-brought-up dogs used to go to school, just like you do now. Every morning when they arrived for lessons, they had to take off their tails and hang them on their pegs. One day there was a big fire at the school, and the teacher told all the dogs to hurry, to just grab any tail on the way out of the school and put it on, they would sort it out later. But, in fact, they never did sort it out, and so now when dogs meet each other, they aren't actually sniffing each other's bottoms, they are looking for their rightful tails.' A sweet story, and if you ever have young children around, it might just come in handy one day.

Throughout the introductions, Stephen, as usual, had sat on the floor with the new arrival between his legs, holding him loosely. Without sight, this puppy's other senses were working overtime. His head was up to allow his twitching nose to catch as many smells as possible. Most of the dogs, in turn, had touched him, sniffing an ear or nudging his chest. Babe had briefly licked his face. Each contact went through him like an electric shock: not being able to see it coming must have been terrifying, yet his stumpy little tail was still wagging.

'Stephen, he's so brave, he breaks my heart.'

'It's going well so far.'

'What's his name?'

'Stevie. As in Stevie Wonder, because he's blind and he's black. Rafael chose it. His owners hadn't named him, that says a lot, doesn't it?'

'Well, if he stays, the name goes.'

By the end of the day, there was no doubt that he was staying. We live in a mainly open-plan space, but that first day, as much as possible, we shut the few doors that there are and let him explore. I crossed my legs and sat on my hands, trying to physically stifle the instinct to run to him every time he headed for a wall. Whenever one of the other dogs approached him, he froze, occasionally produced a small puddle and his little tail wagged like crazy. As in all of the five previous times that we had acquired a new dog, or dogs, the rest of the day was lost: we spoiled the others with treats and made a fuss of the newcomer. Later that same evening, having eaten heartily, he tentatively made his way

from the kitchen to the terrace. We were sitting, discussing all
the potential problems that we might have to face with life with
a blind dog. He bounced towards our voices, bounced off walls
and chairs, but he made it. Less than an hour later, he repeated
the same journey to the terrace without bumping into anything.
Stopping every few seconds, he seemed to be thinking, planning
his next move with the concentration of a chess champion, and
eventually he arrived at his chosen destination without a single
bump.

'Stephen, isn't he incredible? It's as if he's got radar.'

It had to be, didn't it? Laughing, Stephen scooped up the
little thing and kissed the top of his head.

'Welcome to your new home, Radar.'

50

Life with a Blind Dog

For our first four years here we didn't have a television, then we cracked, but only up to a point. We still don't have satellite, choosing to only watch Spanish programmes and therefore continue to improve our command of the language. However, living up to the saying that 'the difference between men and boys is the price of their toys', when we decided to move to La Quinta, Stephen bought a Bang & Olufsen flat-screen TV. It does everything, radio, DVD; it turns through 45 degrees at the press of a phallic control unit; it is the love of his life. Meanwhile, I am in love with the Internet. I can order books, play backgammon with people on the other side of the world, and send and receive messages from friends. The day after we got Radar, we looked to the Internet to see what we could find out about blind dogs. In 0.16 seconds, it came up with 507,000 possible sites; 506,680 were about dogs for the blind. Eventually we found what we were looking for and ordered two books from America about caring for blind dogs.

Radar very quickly learned the layout of the house, it was only changes of level that threw him, or the Hoover suddenly appearing in the middle of the floor, which he would hit his head on. But within a couple of days he could follow us upstairs, though he couldn't get down again. We would find him standing on the edge of a step no more than six inches high but totally stuck, dropping a fat baby paw over the side to try and test the drop. *Step* became a very important word.

'Step, Radar. Step. Step.'

It has become our mantra. It is the instruction that he can move forwards safely, and his trust in us makes me want to cry: hearing it, he just leaps. Now we could put Radar on the roof, say 'step' and, bless him, he would.

He did so well that by the time the books arrived, they were almost redundant. The only real concern we still had was the danger of the swimming pool. Apparently citrus oil was the answer. Dogs, so both books said, hate the smell of citrus; sprinkle citrus oil, ideally lemon, around any area that you want the animal to avoid and the problem is solved, they won't go near it. In contrast, they love peppermint, and a few drops near their beds and water bowls will encourage them to seek them out. Ironically, in this land of oranges and lemons, we covered half of Andalucía looking for lemon oil, but the best we could come up with was orange. Triumphant, we returned carrying it into the house along with the bag of lemons that someone had left hanging on the gate. While Stephen was trying to wrestle the top off the bottle of orange oil, Radar and the others munched their way through the bag of lemons we had left on the kitchen floor. So much for citrus. We have not bothered to try peppermint; if they want to go somewhere they do, without the need for encouragement, and Radar blindly follows.

As feared, yet expected, Radar had his first swim about a week later. Luckily we were both near the pool at the time, and Stephen fished him out in seconds. The next time it happened, a few days later, we were sitting on the terrace, laughing at him trying to chase the twins around the garden. He was having a wonderful time; all our other dogs had realised very early on that there was something different about Radar and, as predicted, they all watched over him. When in the middle of a game they noticed that he was standing in a corner, face to the wall, stumpy tail wagging, playing his solo version of hide-and-seek, any one of them would run over and give him a nudge back in the right direction. On this occasion, it was Piglet who spotted that Radar had cornered himself yet again. Piggy ran to him, nudged him to turn around and then ran back to join the game. Radar followed him eagerly. Unfortunately, Piglet chose the shortcut, over the little mosaic waterfall that trickles down through the rocks and into the pool. He cleared it easily in one bound. Radar didn't. We were out of our chairs and running.

'Jackie, wait.'

'Wait? *Wait?* Have you gone mad?'

'We can't live like this. We have got to see if he can get out on his own.'

He surfaced, spluttering. He had gone in at the deep end and, therefore, was as far away from the steps as was possible. Stephen had to hold me back; every instinct in me was screaming to go to his rescue. All four paws began working frantically, and he made it to one side about halfway along the pool. From there, he doggy-paddled his way along the edge, not that I was expecting back crawl or butterfly, but he made it. The minute the first paw hit the step, he knew that he was safe; you could see it on his face. I ran for a towel and gave Stephen hell for the whole episode, though now I can see that he was right. We had to know. Our dogs have free run of the garden whether we are in or out, and if Radar hadn't been able to get himself out of the pool, all of that would have had to change.

He's only been in once since then. Stephen had left very early one morning for the golf course. I turned over and promised myself another half-hour snooze. A good hour later, I was still totally unconscious when something wet landed on my face. Radar, who had, until that day, never been able to jump onto the bed, had made it. By the trail of water leading from the swimming-pool steps, across terraces, through the house, up the stairs and into our bedroom, it was clear that he had survived another dip.

51

Mystery Solved

I had long stopped wondering about who had dumped the three little shits with us. Pablo was thriving with Lynn and Tony, and the twins were good, sweet-natured dogs who had settled in well. Like their elder brothers and sister, they enriched our lives. Stephen would still worry about the mystery occasionally, like running a tongue around a sore tooth, but I was sure we would never find out, and by now it didn't really matter anyway.

Saturdays are our busiest days, particularly when we have new arrivals in all four houses and only four hours to get them all clean. In theory, people should leave by ten on the morning of departure, but those with evening flights often linger, while the new arrivals should not turn up before two, but often do. This is all very understandable and all very annoying. Between the houses, we have five double and seven single beds, all to be changed even when there has only been one couple staying in a three-bed house. Some, it seems, like to try out all the bedrooms, and why not? Sounds like fun and, after all, they are paying for the privilege.

To achieve this feat of industrial-scale domestic cleaning, we have six cleaners: Lourdes, of course, with her elder sister, Aurora, and Charo, Aurora's sister-in-law, together with Carmensita, Rosa and Miriam – needless to say, they are all related. They work in pairs, and the four eldest each have responsibility for a specific house, of which they are fiercely proud. Early on Saturday mornings, in a part of the basement of La Panificadora, now called the Cueva de Lourdes, where we keep the laundry, there is always a tug-of-laundry war as they argue about what belongs to which house, trying to claim their favourite towels and bed linen.

(The Cueva is so called because Lourdes and her elder sister were born there. Thirty-seven years ago, Aurora, the mother of Aurora, gave birth to the first of her three daughters in this one room. To celebrate this event, the new father went out and bought the new mother her first pair of proper shoes. Until then she had only ever worn homemade woven esparto-grass sandals on her feet. This was in the late 1960s.)

The girls call Saturdays '*los días del supermercado*' (their supermarket days). Anything left in the houses is theirs, and again, it is amazing how people differ. There are times when they are lucky if there is a crust from a loaf and a rotting tomato, though Lourdes's goats are always grateful. Other times, the clients must have gone shopping the day before they left, leaving behind nearly full bottles of whisky and gin and enough food to last a week. Not all is well received. The small pot-bellied black jar with the bright yellow lid is always handed to us with a grimace. They have all now tried Marmite once, and only once. Curious and adventurous in the early days, they now ask for information about the various travel-sized bottles of lotions and potions left in the bathrooms. Lourdes arrived one Monday with very greasy hair, carrying a bottle she had found in Casa Rosa the previous Saturday. She announced that she was not very impressed with English shampoo. It was hand cream. A blotchy Carmensita was equally disgusted by the strength of English skin toner, which, it turned out, was nail-varnish remover. Instructions are not needed for the vast array of pool toys that most of our guests leave behind. By the middle of July, all the girls have enough inflatable dolphins, sharks and whales to open their own aquariums.

We are very lucky, occasionally, when one of the team of cleaners can't make it because between themselves they organise a stand-in. One Saturday about eight months after we had discovered the three little shits, just for that day we had a new girl on the team: Puri, short for Purificación. No more than 20, she was someone that I vaguely recognised but didn't really know. Lourdes introduced her, saying that we certainly knew her father, Sebastian, who was often in Antonio's, which indeed we did. Just after two, as usual, they all arrived back at La Quinta to be paid. As usual, all the dogs greeted them excitedly, but the new girl burst into tears. Everyone looked surprised.

'It's OK, the dogs are all good; they won't hurt you.'

She started sobbing her heart out.

'Lourdes, she's obviously upset by the dogs. Take her outside and I will give you her wages.'

Carmensita remarked that it was strange that she was so upset; her family had always had dogs in the *campo* and Puri had grown up surrounded by them.

It wasn't until the following Monday that we got the full story. Between sobs, Puri had explained that her dog, Luna, had had puppies. It wasn't the first litter; in fact, it was the third, and Puri's father was furious at his daughter's carelessness. I felt like telling him it could have been a lot worse: Puri was an extremely pretty girl. When the pups were just under four weeks old, she came home one day to find them gone. Her father claimed that he had found a good home for them, but he refused to say where, and for all those months she believed that he had killed them. Her tears were of delight, not sadness (common around here), because two of the three puppies were alive and well after all. By this time she was all smiles, until Lourdes told her that in fact not only two, but all three puppies were alive and well – the third was thriving, too – then, loads more tears.

52

Ocho

We have a beautiful big old iron bell, complete with clanger, fitted to the wall by the front gates. It is totally redundant; the dogs let us know if someone is approaching long before anyone reaches it. Something started them off one morning in mid-August. I peered through the pantry window to see a typical white *campo* van driving away. Nothing unusual in that; our drive is often used as a turning point on the narrow road between the village and the coast. For the next hour, one or another would bark every few minutes. This was unusual – something was obviously unsettling them. In August, they do not behave as if they are mad dogs or Englishmen, and move around as little as possible in the heat of the midday sun. It wasn't until calm old Charly started to butt his head against my thigh and whimper that I realised something was wrong. I walked towards the front gates and saw that someone had dumped what appeared to be an enormous dusty, dirty grey rubbish bag in our driveway. As I got closer, there was a slight movement – the bin liner was Cyclops; it slowly lifted its head and looked at me through one weeping eye.

Both Niña and Tintin were in a bad way when we took them in, but nothing compared to this. It was tied to our gate by a piece of thin wire threaded through the tatty piece of dirty old rope that had obviously served as a form of collar. We didn't need another dog. If there had been an available pile of sand, I would have buried my head in it immediately. Instead, I did the human equivalent: turned heel and fled inside. For the next 20 minutes, I pottered around, pretending that it hadn't happened or perhaps I had just imagined it. After all, it was only last week that I had put the milk in the oven and the casserole in the fridge; I was definitely beginning to have 'senior moments'. I went to check again. No such luck, it was still there; in fact, it hadn't moved as much as an inch. Slowly I edged towards the gate and, without taking my eyes from the huge lump of dog, I carefully untwisted the wire. Then, against all my natural instincts, I started jumping up and down like a madwoman, shouting at it to go away, go home! I kicked and rattled the gates, picked up a small stone from the path and bounced it inches from his nose. Slowly and painfully it stood up, took one faltering sideways step, then its legs folded under it. It was midday, the temperature was in the high thirties and still climbing, though luckily the drive was still partly shaded by the tall cypress trees. The logic in my head was telling me to ignore it. Ignore it, and it would go somewhere else to seek food and water. The emotion in my heart was saying, 'What the hell are you doing? Get it some water, at least – and quickly.'

I manoeuvred a water bowl through the narrow slats of the gate, filled it and sat back watching the matted mass. It shuffled forwards on its belly and drank the lot, then had seconds and thirds. Good, now it would have the strength to be on its way. Throughout this, Tintin, our four-legged pogo stick, was on the high wall above the gates, watching with interest. T.T. does not have a nasty bone in his body or thought in his mind. These days he just wants to meet and love as many people and animals as possible, and he was whining with the frustration that he was separated from a potential new friend.

Stephen called from the golf course, full of the joys of life – he had had a good round; in fact, his best round for over a year, so there was a distinct possibility that we would have to make more room for yet another hideous trophy in the top of the airing cupboard.

'I'll be home within the hour, let's go out for dinner tonight. How about somewhere on the beach?'

'Great, but we'll have to sort the dog out first.'

'What's happened? Which one now?'

'It's not one of ours; someone has tied the saddest-looking thing you have ever seen to our gate.'

'I'm on my way.'

It was more than 18 months since we had taken on Radar, and since then we had regularly seen stray dogs on our travels, most distressingly wandering along the hard shoulders or, even worse, the central reservations of motorways. But enough was enough, and as Stephen accelerated and I looked over my shoulder, wishing them luck as they disappeared into the distance, I consoled myself with the fact that we had done more than our fair share for the abandoned dogs of the area. Having seven dogs, and no intentions of having any more, *ocho* – number eight – had become our generic name for any stray that we saw:

'There was a really pretty *ocho* on the golf course today.'

'Stephen, there were some gypsy boys in the market this morning; they were trying to sell the tiniest puppies from a cardboard box. They were far too small to be away from their mum – the puppies, I mean, not the boys. There was almost an *ocho*, there were four of them, but one in particular looked so weak, I was very tempted.'

I went back to the gate to top up the water bowl and, without getting up, it attempted a wag of its badly docked tail. Now the sun was overhead, there was no shade in the driveway. Knowing that Stephen was on his way and that this poor thing wasn't going to go anywhere of its own accord, I opened the gate and laid a trail of ham in little pieces towards the porch. Weak as he was, he was starving and had an instinct for survival. Shakily, he followed the trail and collapsed in the shade of the porch.

Propped against the wall, sitting beside him, talking quietly and stroking gently, it was the first opportunity for me to really have a good look at him. He didn't have ears. Where they should have been was ragged, rimmed, thick old scar tissue. The one eye that could open was brown and bloodshot. The other, covered in burrs and grass seeds, had matted into a Brillo pad; a trickle of yellow pus oozed from the corner. I knew the expression, but until then had never met anything that you could describe as having paws the size of dinner plates. Though his claws were short, both dew claws were broken and hanging and his pads scarred and blistered. His grey-black coat was filthy and seemed to be home to half the insect life of Andalucía. After a few minutes, he shuffled himself around, put his huge head across my legs, sighed deeply and began to slobber and snore, completely ignoring the hundreds of flies that crawled all over him.

Stephen's mother always buys me what turn out to be my favourite clothes, things that often I would not choose for myself and sometimes put on grudgingly then never take off, and that day I was wearing a pair of black Betty Barclay jeans that she had said were 'just me'. They were very just me, but they were swiftly becoming infested with all that this mutt had brought with him.

So this is how Stephen found us, sitting on the floor of the front porch. He left the car at the edge of the drive and slowly walked towards us, stopping about six feet away with a wry smile.

'What a state.'

'I can see that, and the dog doesn't look too good either. We'll take him to Rafael when he opens at five.'

Meanwhile we left him outside in the shade with more food and water, and I went for a very long, very hot shower.

Stephen easily lifted the dog into the car – he showed no resistance – and then carried him into the surgery. Dolores, Rafael's wife, was on duty together with Victoria, a young, newly qualified vet who had joined their practice earlier that year. Victoria is extremely attractive, so much so that since then, if one of the animals as much as sneezes, Stephen starts muttering about taking it to the vet just to be on the safe side. The minute they saw the dog, they both had tears in their eyes. He stood placidly, swaying slightly while they examined him. With a check of his teeth, Dolores said he was about six, maybe seven years old, so about the same age as Charly. He looked 90 if he was a day.

'He's badly dehydrated, obviously underweight, but worse: long-term undernourished. Until we can get that eye open, I won't know how bad it is, and as for the state of his coat . . .' She trailed off.

'What happened to his ears, Dolores?'

'It's common in the *campo*, although the practice is dying out now, thank goodness, but at one point all working dogs had their ears and tails cut as puppies. Though I have never seen such a bad case; this looks like it was done with a blunt penknife.'

'Dolores, we are going to have to try and find a home for him. If you need to shave him in places to get the worst out, it might be better to do it all over; otherwise he'll look more moth-eaten than ever.'

'Leave him with us for a couple of hours; we will see what we can do. Come back at eight.'

The one working brown eye watched us as we walked away, and he sighed deeply, as if to say, 'I knew that was too good to be true.' From outside, I peered back through the window: he was still watching the door; he was still swaying. The empty doorway seemed to mark the end of another short chapter of what seemed to have been a hard life. Yet he stood there, I suppose he had no choice, and looked resigned to face whatever life was going to throw his way next. Although huge, he looked weak, pathetic and so very vulnerable.

We went to a nearby tapas bar, ordered a bottle of wine, chewed absentmindedly through the ham and olives, and sat staring into our glasses in silence. My mind was racing. We already had too many dogs. How was I going to even begin to explain that I had fallen instantly in love with this one? Stephen broke the silence.

'Well, where do we start? The rescue charities, I suppose, and there is a chap I play golf with sometimes, Brian, he has a lot of land and has built a special compound for all the strays he has taken in. I think he has about a dozen.'

'But they don't live with him, do they? In the house, I mean, or lie by the fire at night, or get to smell what's cooking in the kitchen, have passing cuddles, pats and strokes all day.'

'Well, no, but he would have a much better life than he has obviously been used to.'

'Stephen . . . I think you would agree that you are totally responsible for the fact that we now have seven dogs, wouldn't you?'

'Yes, I suppose so.'

'Well, it's my turn now. I really, really want to keep him.'

As usual, my timing was lousy: he had a mouthful of wine, which he inhaled and almost choked on.

'He's the size of a small horse.'

'Yes.'

'He's probably never been inside a house and won't be house-trained. Can you imagine the size of the . . . ?'

'Probably. And, yes, I can.'

'You heard what Dolores said: he might only have the use of one eye.'

'That's one more than Radar.'

'He might be a cat killer.'

'True, that would be a problem.'

'We don't need another dog.'

'That is also most certainly true. Look, he's a big dog and therefore probably halfway through his life, which doesn't appear to have treated him that well so far. We could change all that. I know it doesn't make sense. I can't explain it. There is just something so sad yet so gentle and brave about him, but something more than that. I feel . . . I can't explain it, but I feel that I *know* him. I really want us to keep him. Please.'

'OK.'

'And another thing, he . . . did you say OK?'

'Yes, I said OK. So come on, it's nearly eight, how appropriate. Let's go and see how Ocho is doing.'

Back at the vet's, there was a big shiny black dog sitting under the grooming table with the hot-air blower ruffling its coat. Dolores was at her desk doing paperwork, but there was no sign of Ocho. She smiled as we walked in.

'Doesn't he look better? It took the two of us two hours with the curry comb and a whole bottle of shampoo, but he was so good: he didn't complain once, and we must have hurt him at times. I have rarely met such a sweet-natured creature.'

Confused, we looked under the table again. It couldn't be – but it was. Ocho wasn't greyish; he was jet black, with a white blaze down his chest and white front paws, and his bad eye was now open and clear. Hearing our voices, he had stood up and was wagging what was left of his tail. We let him out of the canine hairdryer and he immediately came and sat quietly at our feet. I looked down at him, and our eye contact was electric.

'Finding a home for him won't be easy. I will put a notice on our pinboard and ask around, but most people want younger and certainly smaller dogs. One of the animal-rescue charities may have a kennel space, though I doubt it.'

'We have decided to keep him.'

She burst out laughing. 'I just don't believe you two, but I couldn't be more happy. He is a very lucky old boy.'

We chose a collar and asked about vitamin tablets, which Dolores agreed would give him a much-needed boost.

'What do we owe you, Dolores?'

'Twelve euros: seven for the collar and five for the vitamins.'

'And for the rest?'

'That was only time, and if you are prepared to give yours, we will gladly give ours. There is no price on saving an animal's life and giving it a loving home.'

This was not the first time we had encountered Rafael and Dolores's kindness and generosity towards animals. Before the motorway link from Málaga was completed, the coast road took all the traffic and was very busy. We were filling up the car in a garage on the outskirts of Nerja when there was the most dreadful scream that seemed to freeze time. The garage forecourt was busy and everyone turned, seemingly in slow motion, in the direction of the noise. Then Stephen and another man were running, dodging the traffic and bending by something in the grass on the far side of the road. Even now when I remember that scream, I get goose pimples. It had sounded human. Seconds later, Stephen was back.

'Get in quickly, we need Rafael.'

Stephen double-parked outside, and I ran in. There were three or four people with assorted animals in the waiting room, and the door to the surgery was open.

'Rafael, a dog has been hit on the main road. Can you help?'

Without a word, he grabbed his Gladstone bag and was in the car in seconds. It could not have been more than five minutes since the accident by the time Rafael was kneeling at the dog's side, but we were too late: the pretty young pointer was dead. We drove Rafael back to his surgery at a more sedate pace and asked to pay for his time. He refused any payment, saying that it was just a shame he couldn't have helped.

We took Ocho home. The minute we opened the back door of the Land Rover, he jumped in without help. Despite still being very weak, he was determinedly going wherever we were, and the fact that he was now clean, less dehydrated and could see out of both eyes had obviously given him a little more energy and confidence.

We knew that this was going to be our biggest challenge so far. Not only was Ocho the same age and slightly larger than Charly, he was also an unneutered male: two sets of doggie balls in the same house had great potential for problems. Luckily, he was too weak to show any signs of aggression: he flopped in a corner and let the others sniff and investigate. Charly looked less than impressed, but that was normal. It was only after a couple of weeks that the tensions arose. Ocho was getting stronger and more confident by the day, although we had never heard him make a single sound and were beginning to wonder if we now had a mute dog to go with the blind one. He certainly wasn't deaf; he learned his new name within days and would come, sit and lie down when instructed, but, of course, only in Spanish, so we got used to giving instructions in two languages. Combined with the hand signals that we always use to accompany each instruction, it wasn't long before we had eight bilingual dogs. He had obviously, as Stephen had predicted, never been inside a house. He tiptoed around the rugs on the floor as if they were landmines and sat watching television for hours. But not once did he pee or poo inside. This was in contrast to his approach to the garden, which was to bulldoze through and mark everything.

Then the growling started: whenever the two big ones came near each other, which in general they both tried to avoid, there would be much growling and baring of teeth. The first time they fought I was terrified; we were all in the garden, and never having seen two big dogs clash before, I really believed they were going to kill each other. Luckily they were quite near Stephen, who was watering plant pots at the time, and the hosepipe on full blast quickly split them up. Three similar incidents and our minds were made up: one set had to go, and on the principle of 'last in first off', we booked Ocho in to see Rafael. It has worked. Although not yet firm friends, he and Charly now rub along together quite happily, and the others, who had never had a problem from day one, adore him.

Claudia, who I am sure has grown up believing she is a dog, uses Ocho as a walkway. She jumps onto his broad back and sits with her paws tucked around his neck until he reaches her chosen destination and then goes her own way. This is her third change of affection; after accepting Domingo's initial nannying, she moved her attention to Radar. They began to sleep together, and we expected them to announce their engagement any day. I thought the delay was due to the choice of ring; she is definitely a big-diamond sort of girl. Radar's enthusiasm cooled when she began to climb trees. One minute she was there, the next she was gone: very confusing for a blind dog. Meanwhile, Pavarotti and Pantoja treat Ocho with the tolerance and disdain they reserve for the rest of their canine family.

53

Don't Even Think About It

Of course, it was stupid to even think about it, let alone allow, even encourage it to happen. But Claudia grew into such an affectionate, adorable cat that we couldn't resist. Most afternoons, before siesta, we stroll around the garden and inspect the progress of the plants. Things grow so quickly in this climate that there are literally day-to-day changes. A bamboo, no more than knee-high when planted, reached twenty feet fewer than three years later. Sapling lemon trees and the grapefruit bush are laden with fruit, we grow our own delicious stumpy bananas, and jasmine invades the terrace. To the left of the driveway, where we have no irrigation system, we have planted what has turned into a brutally spectacular cactus garden. Until moving here, I had never been a cactus fan. My mother always had three or four in pots on kitchen windowsills, and I swear they didn't grow, flower or change. She used to dust them; they were the living dead of the plant world.

The dogs have always joined us on our wanders; we Pied Piper our way around. Ocho picked up this habit very quickly, possibly encouraged by the pockets full of dog treats that we always carry. He has turned into a foodie. The six or seven years of his famine have resulted in a dog that can't say no. To begin with he needed fattening up, but now he needs to enrol in Weight Watchers. Ocho has become Ochissimo. Javier recently described him as the 4x4 of the dog kingdom. He has also remembered, or more probably learned for the first time, how to play, how to bark and how to just have fun. Number eight, these days, is a small shaggy Shetland pony masquerading as a dog. He loves life and hates the flies that he used to ignore; in fact, now he has the energy to take them as a personal insult.

Claudia has also always accompanied us on our *vueltas*, demanding more than her fair share of treats. We were halfway round the garden late one afternoon when I casually mentioned that it would be wonderful if she had kittens. We had already discussed that it was nearing the time to take her to Rafael for her operation, and I expected Stephen to dismiss my romantic musings in a flash. But he did it again.

'Yes. Why not?'

I didn't say another word. Time went on, and a trip to the vet for Claudia was not mentioned again.

Soon after her first birthday, I was hanging out the washing when a gigantic ginger tom appeared. It rubbed around my legs and refused to be shooed away. Two hours later, it had been joined by a rather fetching tabby and our neighbour's jet-black cat from hell. By the following morning, a small black-and-white moggie with a scabby, runny nose and a sore paw had added its number to the throng. They all had one thing in common – *huevos*. At last, the penny dropped. Claudia was ready to meet her suitors.

Back in the house, I took my maternal responsibilities seriously. I sat little Clouds on my lap and explained the facts of life. I agreed with her that it was more than a touch disappointing that between all four of them there was not a guitar, a bunch of flowers or even a box of chocolates in sight. I promised that whoever she chose, we would respect her decision and love him like our own, but urged her to give serious thought to the tabby. She jumped off my lap, stretched lazily with the flexibility of a gymnast and, after a shy, backward look, walked outside. Forty-eight nail-biting hours later, she was back. Ignoring my outrage, she refused to answer a single question.

Was she or wasn't she? A Google search gave me the facts, but not the information I was looking for: only Claudia could do that. Gestation for cats is normally between 58 and 64 days, it said. First-time mothers usually have between two and four kittens, it said. OK, if she was pregnant we were looking at the very end of April or the first week in May, and she would probably, if conforming to the average, have three babies.

She couldn't possibly be pregnant. She was climbing trees as usual, eating as normal, playing rough-and-tumble with the pack and showing no signs of cravings for charcoal, bitter chocolate or pickled onions. She hadn't even put on weight – and then, suddenly, almost overnight, she blossomed. Her skinny little frame remained just that, but she developed a low-slung bumbag, and although I would not have thought it possible, she became more affectionate than ever.

Back to the Internet. Cats rarely have their kittens where you would expect or want them to. Many leave home to have their litter, especially if they perceive a threat to the offspring. Well, no problem there, no threat here; Claudia thought I was her mother, and all eight dogs loved her as much as she loved them. Eight dogs. Would she suddenly consider that to be a threat? I became obsessed with the possibility that she would go away to have her kittens and, without me there to help her, die in the process.

By the beginning of May I was jumping every time she made a sound, whereas Claudia seemed to be on Valium. She was following her usual routine, only at a slightly slower pace and with a big smile on her face. Our house, normally rather minimalist in style, looked like the depot of a famine-relief charity. I had put old rugs, jumpers and blankets on every available surface and in every possible corner. In the spare bathroom there were piles of fluffy towels, sterilised water, dental floss and newly sharpened nail scissors. (Dental floss was apparently the perfect thread to cut the umbilical cord if the mother was not able to bite through it herself.)

I now knew about such things. I had surfed for hours, learning to be the perfect midwife to our feline friend, and almost frightened myself to death in the process, reading all the potential dangers and horror stories. Stephen had every confidence in her, saying I was overreacting as usual and that for Claudia, a typical *campo* moggie, it would be like shelling peas. As a mother, it was an expression I hated.

'When is the next full moon?'

'I don't have a clue. Why do you ask?'

'I've just been speaking to Javier; he says that Clouds will have her kittens on the day of the next full moon.'

Locally, the moon's activities carry great weight. Crops are planted when it is waxing and, months later, harvested only as it wanes. Many years before, Lourdes was appalled that I was going to have my hair cut during a waxing moon.

'Jackie, *por favor*, you are wasting your money: your hair will grow again so quickly, wait a week.'

She also advised waxing my legs when the moon is waning – nothing growing – it would last much longer. I guess every country has its old wives' tales.

54

4 May

Our study, lined with books and photographs, painted a pale Andalucían blue, is our animals' official bedroom. There are eight wicker baskets with plump cushions hugging the walls and, with the exception of Domingo ('My basket is my basket, the one in the corner, green cushion and away from the door. Mine. OK?'), they all seem to pick and choose at random. It works well during the day and for all of five minutes after we have gone to bed. Then they begin to creep up the stairs. Niña is always first, she favours the bath mat, then Tintin heads for the shower. Babe and Piglet drop to their bellies, shuffle under our bed and still sleep entwined. Radar wanders around until he corners himself and sleeps where he drops. Ocho, the self-appointed protector, dominates the top landing and competes with Stephen to see who can snore the loudest. Only Charly and Domingo, our first two and the best trained, stay in the study in their baskets overnight.

Stephen bought Claudia a foam igloo cat bed when she was no more than three months old. We made a space for it under the computer, between a couple of the wicker baskets. I didn't think that she would ever use it; in my experience, cats always sleep where they want to. She loved it from day one.

Early evening on 4 May, I was sitting at the computer when she strolled into the study, gave an even louder than usual purr, rubbed herself against my legs and climbed into her igloo. Her first kitten arrived within minutes. It was Charly who alerted me; he stood beside me and shoved his nose into Claudia's tent. He reversed rapidly, sneezed, chuffed and lay down only inches away with his tail wagging like crazy. I watched fascinated as she rolled onto her side, lifted a back leg and allowed a tiny slimy sack, about the length of my little finger, to slip into our world. Immediately she stood and began to lick it, but within seconds she lay down again and produced another. I was ready for this. If newborns arrive in quick succession, the new mother may not be able to cope. It is essential to ensure that the kitten's airway is clear; usually, all that is necessary is to gently wipe its face with a sterilised towel dipped in cold, pure water.

It took me less than a minute to run to the bathroom, collect my emergency kit and be back at Claudia's side, but I was too late. Charly had beaten me to it. With his head inside the igloo, he was as intent as the new mum, licking blood-smeared mucus from the second kitten. Claudia settled down with her new babies and Charly went outside for some air. On his way, he had obviously told the others of the news. He looked so proud that I kicked myself for not having bought him some cigars to hand out. Two by two, as dictated by Noah, the dogs came to visit. They all stuck their noses into the crib and gently licked the kittens, while little Claudia purred like a lioness and smiled contentedly.

The drama, or rather the lack of it, was over. Claudia had pushed the two newborns towards her teats and they were suckling happily. Just over an hour later, I had almost finished sending the news around the world to our animal-loving friends when, with equal lack of fuss or fanfare, number three arrived. This time Clouds had five or six minutes to clean and welcome it before the fourth and smallest of the lot made her debut.

We sat on the terrace late that night, celebrating the arrival of four perfect kittens and watching that night's full moon reflecting off the sea. For Claudia, still smiling though asleep with her babies, it did seem to have been rather like shelling peas.

As we suspected, she has turned out to be an excellent mother. Her firstborn, a boy, was followed by three girls. Growing up surrounded by dogs, Claudia has passed her acceptance to her kittens, who within a month were more or less mobile and totally fearless. This time it was Babe who became second mum to the new arrivals. The first time one of the babies fell two steps down the terrace stairs, she was there in seconds and, gently picking it up by the scruff of its neck, carried it back to Claudia.

Rafael approved. He pointed out that she had produced exactly what the continuation of the species demanded: three childbearing females and a strong, healthy firstborn male to sire them. I bit my tongue and smiled. In memory of my father, a firstborn boy followed by six sisters – so I suppose my grandmother did even better than Claudia in that respect – we have called him William, and the name seems to sit comfortably with him. He also fulfilled the dream: he is the most perfect Mediterranean tabby with the Cleopatra eyeliner and charcoal stripes that match across his front legs. The youngest two of Claudia's girls, Luna and Paloma, are happily living with Javier, Rosario and our godchildren. William and his sister Paintbox live with us (or do we live with them?). Paintbox, commonly known as P.B., has a little bit of every cat colour possible, which is not helpful as Claudia still refuses to name the father. Perhaps she is planning to write her own book one day, although she knows I disapprove of kiss and tell.

55

Any Excuse for a Party

By 15 May, life had returned to normal. It is one of Spain's many saint's days, celebrated with the people's usual enthusiasm for a party. The saint on this occasion is San Isidro, the patron saint of farmers and labourers, who lived in Madrid in the twelfth century. Although poor, he took in passing waifs and strays and shared the little food he earned with anyone in need.

Nerja celebrates this day with a procession that officially leaves the Balcón at midday – but add an hour and you'll still be there on time. It is led by gleaming horses with manes plaited in the green-and-white colours of Andalucía; they kick their heels like a group of Tiller Girls. The riders are, in general, men that you could walk past in the street and not notice, but on that day, in their short jackets, striped trousers and polished boots, be they 16 or 60, they all look like George Clooney. Beautiful girls ride side-saddle behind them; posing with an attitude of superiority, they lift their heads and adjust the frills of their skirts, seemingly oblivious to the flashing lights of the tourist cameras.

Following behind are the floats. We are often invited to join a family float and have never refused. Pulled by polished, powerful oxen, these carts are laden with several generations. It is a strange contrast to see a baby buggy strapped to the side of an ox cart, while an old lady in black carves thin slices of *jamón* from a haunch hanging from the canopy.

Behind and alongside these carts walk the rest of the family. Dressed in their geranium frills, they sing, they dance and they laugh as they call out to friends in the crowd. When a youngster shows signs of wilting, it is passed, over heads and through willing hands, to the nearest float. The journey on a normal day would take less than five minutes by car. On 15 May it takes three hours, punctuated by pauses for exchanges of food between fellow revellers and *sevillana* dancing.

Eventually everyone arrives under the pines at the picnic site by the caves. The normal assortment of fairground stalls sell their wares and ply their rides. The music that comes from the bars and *casetas* (tented restaurants) set up for that day makes the ground throb and the people dance. In keeping with the fact that San Isidro was the labourers' saint, beneath the feminine frills of flamenco dresses, we wear sturdy, handmade leather boots. The party continues long into the night; children are cuddled until they sleep, then watched over by proud grandparents.

It is Nerja's biggest day, one that we always look forward to, and probably the day when I feel most Spanish. The dress helps, of course, and with my dark hair and tanned skin I could be mistaken for a native – the only give-away is the green eyes; sadly I am most certainly not a black-eyed beauty. As the parade snakes through the streets, it is watched by hundreds of tourists, and we used to stand on the sidelines with them. Now, we are part of their family and they are part of our soul.

56

Life in the Fast Lane

I am not talking about our lives here; we gratefully left the fast lane behind in London. In fact, we cheated by calling her Fastlane; she was actually in the middle lane when Stephen spotted her. He was on his way back from watching his beloved Málaga FC, driving on the motorway that now passes only a few kilometres from our still sleepy village.

Dusk was settling as he approached the final tunnel before our turn off, and I can guarantee that he would have been travelling at a speed that he would not admit to me. A small black speck in the middle lane seemed to be moving slowly from right to left. His friends' animated conversation about Málaga's win fell silent as he slammed on the brakes and pulled the car up sharply on the hard shoulder. At this point, were Stephen telling the story, he would go into great detail about the superb engineering of a Land Rover's advanced braking system. All I know is that he stopped. Very quickly. As he ran back down the hard shoulder and came level with his quarry, it disappeared between the wheels of a transit van, but emerged untouched as it passed.

We will never know how a tiny kitten, less than a month old, was wandering around in the middle lane of a remote stretch of motorway. Her survival seemed so incredible that we elevated her name to Fastlane. When Stephen got home and said he had a present for me, I was surprised. It was a Sunday, normal shops were closed and he knew that I would not be seen dead even drinking from a Málaga FC coffee mug, let alone wearing one of those hideous nylon football shirts. She was shaking, filthy and suffering from such a bad eye infection that we feared that we would have a blind cat to keep Radar company. Luckily, her left eye cleared with the drops that she hated, so we now have a Cyclops with a tendency to tilt her head to the right in order to focus. What she lacks in sight she makes up for in vocabulary; she chats away about everything from her favourite foods and when they should be served to her feelings about being evicted from our bed.

Our cleaners were appalled that we would even consider keeping a black cat as a pet. In Spain, a black cat crossing your path is considered unlucky. It led to an interesting exchange of superstitions. They agreed that thirteen was unlucky, being the number of attendees at the Last Supper, but they had no fear of Friday the thirteenth (here it is Tuesday the thirteenth that is unlucky). I didn't think that even in this most Catholic of countries, it would be possible to link bananas with religion. I was wrong. No one in the village would dream of cutting a banana – instead, they break them with their fingers. A cut cross-section of a banana represents cutting the cross; therefore, a Spanish fruit salad, like many of its creators, is a rather chunky affair.

Enough is Enough

The arrival of Fastlane, our ninth cat, and Ocho, our eighth dog, also marked our eighth year of living here. We had acquired seventeen animals, which worked out, on average, as being soft – some may say stupid – at least every five months. All of this motley crew of mutts and moggies had been orphaned or abandoned. We had too many animals, but we had the time and space for them, and also the feel-good factor of knowing that without us, they would all most likely be dead.

This should really be the end of this story. Our lives had settled into a gentle routine; we had our tasks and chores; as anyone who owns one old house, let alone four, will appreciate, there is always something to do. We had finally achieved a happy balance between work and play. All the animals were calm and settled; their early teething problems – sometimes literally – were over.

'I met a really nice woman today when I dropped some stuff off at the C.A.S. Shop, you know where I mean, the charity place that helps abandoned animals.'

'I thought that was our house.'

'I said I had some spare time and offered to help out. You don't mind, do you?'

'Of course not, though I really can't picture you working in a charity shop, somehow, no matter how good the cause.'

'Not in the shop. People often find tiny puppies and kittens abandoned, sometimes in the rubbish bins, isn't that awful? I was telling her about Domingo and Claudia, about bottle-feeding them. They are desperate for people to do that, so I gave her our number.'

'More animals?'

'Only for a couple of weeks at a time – well, perhaps five or six weeks at the most, until they can survive on their own and the charity has found a permanent home for them. It probably won't happen, anyway.'

It happened three days later. Karen, the lady that I had met at C.A.S. (the Costa Animal Society), called to ask if we could take two kittens found early that morning in a cardboard box on waste ground. We drove down to the vet used by the charity to collect them. We have always used Rafael's practice since that random first choice and first visit with Charly. We are very happy with him, and, with the exception of Charly ('Vet? I'd rather go to the dentist.'), so are our animals. Expedito is one of the other two vets in town, another lovely man, especially so because he gives his time to the street animals for free. In his reception area there is a huge cage, from which the pleading eyes of unwanted puppies and kittens tug at the heartstrings of the owners of spoiled pooches who only popped in to buy another diamanté-encrusted collar. It often works.

I don't think either of us was prepared for just how tiny our foster babies would be. They looked more like lucky-rabbit-foot key rings than newborn kittens, with protruding ribs, bald feet and flaps of skin yet to become ears, flat to their heads. The two of them fitted easily into the palm of my hand, their eyes tight shut as if they didn't want to see what the world had to offer. We called them Bubble and Squeak; their top ends squeaked and their tail ends bubbled. Thus began the habit of giving them all temporary names. (While it is a very long time since I have observed the Catholic faith, some bits are hard to shake off, and knowing that some will die, at least they die with a name, if not the holy-water bit.) Next came two little puppies the size of small hamsters: one was a golden brown, his brother a pale beige. It was early November; we named them Pumpkin and Parsnip. I spent hours telling them how beautiful they were; what wonderful lives they would have; to be patient, their milk was cooling. I babbled to them all day, thinking that as their eyes were not yet open, the sound of my voice would be comforting. It was many months and many puppies later that I was told that they cannot hear for the first ten or so days of their lives.

Within two weeks of my innocent offer of help, we were in sole charge of two kittens, two puppies and a further puppy, all fewer than ten days old. The last to arrive that month was Sprout, who, thank goodness, sprouted beautifully. It was the beginning of a steep learning curve that was punctuated by highlights and heartaches.

58

The Dog with No Name

Our faces soon became as familiar to Expedito as they had over the years to Rafael and Dolores. So when he called one Friday asking if we could help, I assumed that it would be yet more very small bundles and hoped it wouldn't be too many.

When we arrived at the surgery, it was unnaturally quiet. The waiting room was empty, the cages were open and Expedito was packing papers into his briefcase.

'Thanks for this, it's only until Tuesday, I really appreciate it.'

One weekend a year, the practice closes and a team of professional fumigators blitzes everything. Expedito schedules this well in advance to ensure that all the animals are gone and emergency cover is provided by the other vets. What was not on his schedule was the puppy that he found tied to the front door of his reception that morning. He opened a side door and a whirlwind of almost-spaniel sped towards us. As her speed increased, she lost traction on the marble floor and, covering the last few feet sliding on her back, she arrived at Stephen's feet with her legs in the air. It was love at first sight.

'Hello, silly girl.'

Stephen scooped her up and we turned to leave.

'What are you calling her, Jackie? I need a name for my records.' Stephen had rung a bell with me when he called her silly. When I was a child I had a very pronounced lisp, and my father thought it funny to call me silly, to which I would respond, 'I'm not tilly.' Tilly became my family nickname, and the weekend name for the puppy.

Both our canine and feline family were by this stage totally blasé about new arrivals; the younger ones would pause to give a passing lick and sniff, the elders just rolled their eyes and adopted a 'not again' sort of expression. Tilly was a different matter. At about three months old, she could not and would not be ignored by anyone. She was blessed with the soulful eyes and frothy feathers of a spaniel. Her coat was snow white with perfect black patches, and she had a sprinkling of ginger freckles over her plump little upturned nose. Because she was still so young, she had not yet grown into her ears, which hung down to her knees and would have made a bloodhound jealous.

Several things soon became clear. She was probably a Christmas puppy whose batteries were showing no signs of running out. The pads of her paws were soft and baby pink, indicating that she had lived indoors. This was further supported by her first time in the garden, where she bounced around the lawn as if it were a giant green trampoline and ate half a dozen carnations in about ten seconds. In the house, she could do laps of the living room without touching the floor, using chairs, the sofa and a long coffee table to complete the circuit. She had most definitely been living the life of an only child. Young animals, like children, learn how to behave towards both their elders and their peer group by experience. Tilly showed no respect for anyone. Charly and Ocho were appalled by her lack of manners; Niña and Babe, I suspect, were simply just jealous of a younger, prettier girl in the house.

The weekend, like Tilly herself, flew by. On the night before we were due to take her back, she was tearing around the garden and we both were dreading the idea of locking her back in that cage. The following morning, it was amazing how many things we urgently needed to do, little jobs long delayed that suddenly had to be done. Expedito's receptionist called to remind us we had a puppy to return, we hadn't forgotten?

'That was the vet. They are ready for Tilly.'

'You had better take her then.'

'You take her; I'll cry, and so will she.'

'She's not going anywhere, is she?'

'It's up to you.'

'No, it's not.'

She is almost four now, and her weekend name still suits her. She is still a very Silly Tilly. What I didn't consider at the time was our surname, which also suits her: Tilly Todd, our ninth dog.

59

Ignorance – Not Always Bliss

I am sure that everyone has had an event in their lives that they have approached with happy, innocent ignorance, then, years later, thought, 'How did I do that?' We had hand-reared both Domingo and Claudia, but, when fostering, rather like looking after a friend's children, you worry more about them than your own. With those first five, we were as nervous as first-time parents when we set about our task, fretting over their every movement and expression. If they were awake, they were hungry. If they were asleep, they were dead. Was the milk too strong? The milk must be too weak. Then there were the practicalities. What goes in must come out, and they have to be licked to encourage them to poo. Once you have a tiny animal that in an ideal world should still be with its mum, you have to provide every service. Stephen refused point blank (I can't understand why), but luckily Domingo came to the rescue again. His reward for his services was to finish any milk left in the bottle.

We had bottles of every size, syringes for those that wouldn't suckle and, as a last resort, a very fine tube to deliver the milk down their throats and straight into their tummies. Our success rate was high, but some, of course, died, and every loss hit us so hard. There was also the frustration of ignorance, not only ours, but also the vet's. We had no knowledge of the backgrounds of new arrivals, their ages or how long it was since they had been

233

abandoned. Puppies open their eyes at about 14 days old, so we worked backwards from there and chose birthdays for them. Some arrived with their umbilical cords still attached. The cord would fall away within a day or two, and I always felt sad to think that their mum wasn't around to witness that first milestone. The Internet was helpful in some areas. For example, a site detailing the hand-rearing of a litter of American bulldogs talked about using tinned evaporated milk rather than the powdered formula and that was a huge success. It did produce pups that looked like baby sumo wrestlers for their first few weeks, but as soon as they were mobile they ran the weight off, and meanwhile, that puppy fat gave them the much needed safety net if they went off their food for a day. However, when we were looking for possible causes of specific symptoms, the various sites began by talking about breeds and hereditary problems. As we had never met the mothers (who, at the crucial time, probably hadn't bothered to look behind anyway), we had no chance.

We began to recognise the signs of decline. The larger the litter, the wetter the poor little bugger at the bottom of the pile. This only meant that he or she got washed more often than the rest, which did no harm. But there is another type of wet that seems to come from within and usually signals the beginning of a frighteningly rapid end. Also if a tiny puppy or kitten refuses to eat, it can die within hours. Out of exhaustion and sheer frustration, at four in the morning we have been known to sit pleading, 'Eat. Please eat. Listen, kid, it's eat or die. OK?'

On a more positive note, there are far, far more happy endings than sad ones. Both vets are amazed and impressed at our success, and it is now them that call us for help on the many occasions when a box is left on their doorstep overnight. We have what has become a well-practised routine for new arrivals. They are presented to our own brood as soon as we walk through the door; a quick sniff is all it takes to satisfy their curiosity. They are then settled into the spare bedroom, under an infrared lamp in one of the two cardboard boxes that will be their cots for their first few weeks. We use two boxes to make sure they all get fed. When they are so small, six black puppies, for example, are impossible to tell apart, so after their milk and a quick lick with a flannel, they are transferred into the second box. Within a month they are off the bottles and slurping soft food, a very messy business that results in puppy-washing, floor-mopping and clothes-changing (ours) at least four times a day. The washing machine never stops. Since we began fostering three years ago, we have never had more than ten days without a waif in the house.

The biggest headache, however, is finding good new homes. Our friends, and friends of friends, all now have far more animals that they ever intended. Stephen takes stunning photos that manage to make all of our charges look, on one hand, cute, cuddly and adorable, but also vulnerable and pleading. He then creates 'free-to-good-homes' posters and we tour the restaurants, bars, shops and garages asking for permission to display them. We have found homes this way, but just as often a phone call that promisingly starts with 'I saw the poster in the garage' then goes on to ask if we would take the kittens they found in the middle of nowhere that morning.

We are also in the export business. We have contacts with German, Dutch and Scandinavian animal charities who find homes in their respective countries. Prospective owners have to go through a rigorous process of checks to ensure they are deemed suitable, and then pay for the necessary injections, microchips and flights. We comfort ourselves with the fact that to undergo such a performance such people must really want the animal, but taking a puppy to the airport is one of the saddest ways to say goodbye. Most new foreign owners keep in touch with photos, which is great, and it is funny to see an Andalucían *campo* dog up to his armpits in the Hamburg snow, but we know that we will never see them again. Always, more tears.

60

Thank God for Lourdes

I have probably made light of the work involved in keeping our home clean and sweet smelling with so many animals in residence, and so I should. We could not do it without Wonder Woman, Our Lady of the Hoover.

'This place looks like a bomb hit it.'

'Lourdes is here today.'

'Thank God for Lourdes.'

She has been with us for 12 years now and has seen it all. Puppies pee on just-washed floors, think that the mop is to be chased and chewed and that parts of the garden look better indoors. Kittens climb up her legs, run under her feet and try to prove that a certain toilet paper ad should have used them instead. All she asks for when we have a full house is extra bleach. It is embarrassing to stand at the checkout in the supermarket with a trolley containing ten bottles of bleach, ten packets of baby wipes, twenty tins of Carnation milk, and, if I remember, a stick of bread and some cheese for us.

Lourdes is also a great storyteller, and one of her favourite subjects is Blas, her father. She adores him, but he drives her mad – he is very happily stuck in the past. Recently he asked her to take him to Vélez, a 20-minute drive away, to buy some seed potatoes that he had heard were the best in the area. On the way Lourdes stopped for petrol, telling her father to stay in the car, she would only be a minute. He got out – curiosity had got the better of him, he had never been to a garage before. He had, over the years, upgraded the mule to a moped and bought his cans of petrol from the repair shop in the village. This is Lourdes's account of the conversation that followed:

'Where is your can?'

'Don't need one, Dad, the petrol comes from a pump.'

'Where is the lady?'

'What lady?'

'The lady that just told you that you have chosen unleaded petrol.'

Lourdes chose to ignore this and went inside to pay. When she came back, her father, arms folded, was leaning against the pump.

'Well, thank you, I am sure we will have a safe journey. My daughter is a very good driver you know. It is not really a journey any more, of course it used to be, but what with the new roads, we won't be long. I said to Aurora – that's my wife – that we would be back before lunch. Anyway, bye, nice talking to you.'

Lourdes bundled him into the car, not knowing whether to laugh or cry about the fact that her dad was talking to a petrol pump.

My all-time favourite Blas story is 'The Teeth'. You may remember that before his retirement, Blas was the *acequia* man, in charge and in control of the irrigation channels that run through these valleys. One spring, with a nasty head cold, he was changing the direction of the water flow, bent down over the fast-running water, when he sneezed.

His bottom false teeth shot out of his mouth into the water and disappeared. Soon the whole village knew of his loss and sympathised with the thought of how expensive it would be to replace them. After five months of family savings, that September Blas bought his new teeth. A month later, another village Antonio, who had land almost at the coast, three miles from the last sighting, knocked on their door. He had been harvesting his crop and dug up a bottom set of false teeth entwined in the roots of a potato plant. Blas was delighted; now he had a spare set. They were scrubbed and put in a drawer and that should have been the end of the story . . . but last year, his wife had to have all her bottom teeth removed due to a bad gum infection, and the cost of false ones was, to them, staggering. You are ahead of me now, aren't you? Yes, the teeth were resurrected from the drawer. Aurora refused to wear them. Blas took to placing the teeth in the middle of the dining table at every meal. The traditional Sunday family gathering was abandoned for over a month, there was silence between the grandparents, revolution from the girls and hysterical giggles from the grandchildren. Aurora's Christmas present from her family that year required little thought.

61

Bye Bye Baby

Yet more tears. No matter how good a home they go to, even if it is close and I know that I will see them often, it is always a huge wrench, and I always promise myself that we will never do it again. I know that it hurts Stephen just as much.

This book would go into volumes if I told you all their stories, but here are a few. About two years ago, I began to keep a diary to keep track of their birth dates as far as we could guess (it was important for the timings of vaccinations). It was also important to relate emailed photos of an animal I would swear I had never seen before to the baby we had handed over. At one point we had three kittens, two boys and what turned out to be a girl of the same age found on her own at the side of a rubbish dump. All three were still on bottles when we were invited to a lunch party in a restaurant on the beach, so they came too. A lovely girl on the next table watched as we fed them, asked to hold each of them in turn and then, to our amazement, said, 'I'll take the tabby when it's off the bottle.' There were two reasons for our amazement: we were used to people wanting to cuddle cute, furry little things and then hand them back, but not only had she offered to take one on full time, she had also chosen the kitten that we had nicknamed the 'angry young man'. She actually coined a new word in our household: she had 'cattitude'. So when an email entitled Frankie, with attached photos, arrived a few months later, it took a while to realise that the relaxed, smug, smiling tabby lolling on a cushion was, in fact, our little 'cattitude'.

Our little ugly bug is another good example. A charming Scandinavian man named Thor called one evening. His timing was bad (not his fault, but I was two minutes away from serving supper for six). We left our friends to it, jumped into the car and met him in town to take charge of a small puppy. I wish the stories of how we come to look after small animals were more interesting, but the truth is that probably about 70 per cent are found in rubbish bins. Thor had found just such a bag containing seven puppies. Six were dead, and we were about to take on the only survivor.

Having had a glass or two of wine while cooking, I was struggling as we drove to our meeting point, something I blame Stephen for entirely. I had never met a man named Thor, but probably 20 years ago, Stephen had told me a silly ditty:

> The God of War rode out one day upon his handsome filly.
> I'm Thor, he cried.
> His horse replied,
> You forgot your thaddle, thilly.

So, remembering this, although we were picking up a sick puppy, I was stifling giggles.

Most women say that all babies are beautiful. I disagree. All babies, in my opinion, are little miracles of nature and sources of delight, but many, especially those with little hair, resemble Winston Churchill minus the cigar. Looks don't matter, but in the dusk of evening, it wasn't until we got home that we realised that we had just taken in the ugliest puppy in Andalucía. If you can try, conjure up the image of a lump of black fur with dirty white feet, no more than four inches long, eyes tight shut. Now, just imagine that this lump has been hit by a truck and attacked by a mad hairdresser with a crimping iron.

The usual routine fell into place; she and her bottle of milk came with us everywhere, but instead of the usual oohs and aahs, passing people took one look and carried on passing. Most animals tell us what they should be called within a few days – no, I do not hear voices (yet); it's just that some trait, marking or mannerism fits them. We called her Cruella – there was no point in pretending. It is at this stage that you know who your true friends are. They are, by now, all used to the ever-changing assortment of pretty babes and well practised at making suitable noises. Cruella was a different issue. 'She may grow into her looks.' 'Beauty is only skin deep.' 'Personality is more important.' Our friends tried hard. But another comment proved true: 'the ugly ducklings turn into swans', and while swan might be pushing it a bit, Cruella did indeed grow into an adorable, pretty girl with piercing ice-blue eyes and an astrakhan coat. She was lucky, too: she now lives with Roberto and Sarah, who have the best butcher's shop in town. So Ella, as she is now called, is the butcher's dog.

Another lucky lady is Delilah. One of a litter of four, her name just sort of followed on from her brother, Samson, who was twice the size of his siblings. She was offered a home by a lovely Dutch gay couple who live in the hills above Frigiliana. Their house is enormous, luxurious and has two pools, one for them and one for their dogs. When they took our little golden girl, they already had four abandoned dogs living the lives of totally pampered pooches. We do meet all sorts when looking for homes for the animals, but even I wasn't prepared for the surreal phone call one morning about two days after they had taken her.

'Jackie, darling, it's Eric – Eric, Delilah's mummy. Do you think she is warm or cool?'

'Cold? Eric, it's hot today. Is she ill?'

'No darling, not her temperature, her colours. We can't buy anything for her until we know, so we are keeping her on white at the moment, just to be on the safe side.'

He had been arguing with Dirk, who was sure she was cool, but Eric thought she was warm. As I proved useless in settling the matter, they summoned their colour consultant, and later that week, I was delighted to learn that our little Delilah was warm.

62

What a Cracker

We celebrate Christmas twice in our house, which suits me just fine. I love it. I appreciate the view that it has become too commercial and that the true meaning has been devalued; in fact, I agree. But by the middle of December, I am itching to dust off the decorations and put the carols on at full volume. Our first Christmas in La Quinta, with only six dogs and assorted cats, Stephen, as usual, indulged my child-like excitement and arrived home with a beautiful tree, the last tree we have ever had. We decorated it with lights, glass beads and frosted baubles and went to bed that night happy with our efforts. The animals were more than happy, too; they thought all their Christmases had arrived at once. Wasn't it kind of us to provide the cats with the world's biggest scratching post and to decorate it with shiny footballs covered in glitter, just waiting to be plucked. The dogs took a more practical approach. It was getting rather cold to go out in the middle of the night to find a tree and cock a leg, so their thoughtful masters had moved one indoors for Christmas. It floated out of the house the following morning.

Our first Christmas lunch every year is for our Spanish friends, a traditional turkey with all the trimmings. The big Spanish family meal is on Christmas Eve, but they all thoroughly enjoy the English version, taking particular delight in the bread and cranberry sauces, sage-and-onion stuffing and brandy butter. It is a lunch that lasts until midnight; presents are opened and crackers are pulled. The jokes in crackers are never funny in Spanish as they often involve a play on words that falls totally flat in translation, yet every year we are always asked to explain the joke. It has become as much a part of our Spanish celebrations as satsumas and cava.

One year, in addition to our nine permanent canine housemates, we had a litter of four abandoned puppies. Word had got around, and we seemed to be the first port of call when animals were found dumped on the doorsteps or, worse still, in rubbish bins. These had been left outside the Donkey Sanctuary. The Sanctuary is run by Harriet and is home to about 20 donkeys, mules and horses, giving them a much needed refuge from the abuse of their former lives. Over the years she has also acquired several dogs, a few cats, a couple of roosters and a pot-bellied pig called Henrietta. This does not leave her with the time or energy to bottle-feed tiny puppies every three hours.

Christmas is always busy, the houses always full, and that year, the offer to decorate the houses had been taken up by all four parties. So we were lucky that in the early days the puppies turned out to be some of the easiest babies we had ever had. We woke them for feeds, wiped them with warm flannels and then laid them down on clean towels as they fell asleep in our arms. There was only one girl, jet black and the biggest of them all, with the longest, curliest eyelashes I have ever seen on a dog. Her brothers, another black and two tan-brown with black edges to their eyes, noses and ears, soon overtook her in the growth race, though she always ruled the nursery. In keeping with the season, they were named Holly, Santa, Cracker and Pudding. A wicker hamper arrived from English friends, full of goodies that were stored in the pantry and replaced by the puppies. At about four weeks old, they would stand on their back legs in a line and peek over the top of the basket, looking as cute as, well, a basketload of puppies. In reality, they were planning their escape, and we happened to be right there when it happened. Cracker climbed onto Pudding's shoulders to be high enough to do a front flip out of the hamper. Once out, Santa gave Pudding a leg up, and then the two escapees tugged the leather straps until the whole thing flipped on its side, and chaos times four arrived.

We had always thought that Cracker would be the first to find a home; he was certainly the most handsome. As it happened, Pudding, his smaller brown brother, was the first. At a New Year's Eve supper with friends, we teased a couple with one dog about how lonely it must be for him, that it would be much better for him to have a friend. Amazingly, they agreed; they said they had been thinking the same for some time, and their son, Alejandro, would love another dog. So Alejandro had the pick of the litter and chose Pudding, now called Toffee. We still see Toffee Pudding regularly; he is a happy boy with a very good home. Holly was the next to go, again to a couple who already had a much older dog. The two have become firm friends, and their owners say that Holly has given their older dog a new lease of life.

Holly and Pudding were about seven and eight weeks old when they left us. Three weeks later, despite the posters we always put up and all the other methods we use to try to find good homes, we still had the politically correct black Santa and the handsome Cracker. It was time to take them to Expedito to put them in the cage in his reception in the hope that someone would fall in love with them. We had done it before, we have done it since: it never gets any easier. I always feel so guilty because they just think it is a new game. Our house is always full of people, so a reception area full of people is just more new smells and fun; they don't even notice when we walk away. But I know that at eight that evening, when the practice closes, they will be fed, then taken into one of the cages at the back to spend the night. Perhaps they are fine – they are certainly safe, warm and full. I always hope that they sleep better that first night than we do.

After five days with Expedito, they were still there. He closes for the weekend and so, on Saturday morning, we took them home for two days. Within seconds it was as if they had never been away; they were greeted by nine wagging tails, they knew where the water bowl was and took the swipes of the cats' paws in their stride. There were no accusations, 'why did you do that?' or 'poor me'. They were just glad to be home.

To say 'goodbye, good luck and don't forget we love you' once is difficult. To repeat that process the following Monday is more than twice as bad. That week I created a reason to be in town every day, and I would always lurk outside of the big glass window at Expedito's to see how they were doing. The urge to run in and hug them was almost overwhelming, but I knew that it would only have made me feel better and them worse. Luckily, Santa found a home that week. An elderly Spanish lady with a cast-iron perm marched her recently retired husband into the vet's, pointed to the puppies, told him to choose one, to get out from under her feet and start walking a dog. They thought Cracker was beautiful, so they chose Santa because they felt he would be less likely to find a home. We often meet all three of them happily trotting through town.

Week three. Following another weekend with us, Cracker was again in the cage and this time alone. There is a bell over the door to Expedito's reception that alerts the staff to new arrivals. For two weeks, every time the bell rang the puppies had jumped up, wagging their tails with excitement; they were becoming Pavlov's puppies. In the middle of that week, on the way to meet Stephen for lunch, I made a detour just to see how Cracker was doing. As I sneakily peeked through the window, a woman entered the reception, causing the bell to jangle. Cracker lifted his head from his paws and watched her walk to the desk, but stayed curled up in the corner of the cage.

'What's wrong? You look awful.'

'Cracker's ill.'

'What's wrong with him?'

'He's got a broken heart.'

'It's your heart that will break if we leave him there any longer, isn't it? OK. Ten is a nice round number.'

I ran all the way to the vet's, yanked open the door of the cage and scooped him up.

'Come on, Cracker, we're going home.' As we had said when we got Domingo all those years before, 'one more won't make much difference'.

Epilogue

Never Say Never

We have absolutely no intention to take on any more animals on a permanent basis. However, we do realise that we have lost all credibility with friends and family on that front. Like Charly, they just roll their eyes, but rather than chuff, they mumble 'heard-that-one-before' sorts of expressions. Ten dogs are certainly two handfuls, and each season brings its own demands. On the few rainy days of winter, forty muddy paws are a challenge. We light the wood-burning stove, throw rugs down on the terracotta tiles, then watch as a shagpile carpet grows in front of the fire. Ten dogs in every shade of brown, with some black, white and cream for good measure, compete to see who can take pole position. Charly especially needs the warmth now: the couple of Labrador genes we recognised when he was a puppy have, in old age, caused him to pile on the pounds. The extra weight he carries does not help the arthritis that has crept up on him over the last couple of years. But he still leads a full and happy life, takes his medicine like a man and both Domingo and Tilly are happy to give his watery old eyes a soothing lick every morning. Once the dogs are settled for the evening, the cats appear and fill in the gaps. We don't get a look in. Spring brings moulting time; balls of discarded fur roll across terraces like the tumbleweed from a spaghetti western. The heat of summer creates thirsty dogs. Not for us the sweet little ceramic water bowls with paintings of cartoon bones; we use washing-up bowls and refill them several times a day. As the days cool, it is time for their annual injections. We are the only people we know whose vet does house calls for domestic pets. Rafael lines up ten syringes filled with the right amount of vaccine for the weight of each dog. Seven receive their injections and have their passports stamped without fuss, then we go looking for the wimps. Domingo can always be found shivering in his basket, Babe in the far corner of the pantry with her eyes tight shut; only Tintin changes his bolt-hole every year.

Old age has been less kind to Ocho, perhaps due to his first few years of bad nutrition. In 2009, he was walking across the garden when his back legs collapsed beneath him. Blood tests proved diabetes, and we all had to learn how to cope with it. He began to eat a different diet, away from the other dogs, and the first time we gave him his insulin injection, our hands were trembling. But within a week he regained his energy, stood calmly for his injections without a flicker and actually looked better than he had for quite a while.

Then, early one morning, instead of being one of the first of the pack to follow Stephen into the garden, he stayed on the top terrace. We thought nothing of it until we heard the crash. He is a big boy and he had walked not into as much as through a knee-high ceramic pot overflowing with geraniums that had been in the same place for years. All of our dogs screw up at times; they know it when it happens and they run, they hide and then try to adopt an air of innocence. This time Ocho just stood there surrounded by bits of broken pot and a pile of earth.

'Ocho. What the hell are you . . . Stephen!'

This may sound awful, but Stephen, like the dogs, knows the tone of my voice. That morning, when I called his name, he ran.

'Look at his eyes, they are blue and milky in the middle.'

Ocho stood there. He had locked all four knees and was trying to dig his claws into the floor; he moved not his eyes but his ears towards our voices.

'He can't see.'

'Calm down.'

He couldn't see. Overnight, Ocho had lost his sight.

I guess we were more prepared than most, but it is difficult to watch. We had almost forgotten that Radar was blind, he always coped so well, but it has taken Ocho longer to adjust. I think that for him the issue is more one of loss of pride than loss of sight. He has fallen into the pool four times now; he gets himself out and pretends that he fancied a quick dip. He is now always the back runner on walks and he no longer follows us upstairs. He has always loved his cuddles, any excuse, any time. Now, though, he will not accept cuddles if they come from sympathy. If he could talk, I am sure he would say, 'Poor Ocho? Don't know what you're talking about.'

Last night I didn't know whether to laugh or cry. For more than five years now, both Ocho and Charly have behaved with the appropriate grace of the senior citizens of their pack. They have their own circle of young pups and older followers, they sleep at opposite ends of the terrace, they tolerate each other. Last night, Charly got up. This is no longer an easy feat. He rolled to one side and, putting all of his weight on his front legs, sat for a few moments before steadying himself, regaining his balance and heaving the bulk of his rear end onto almost redundant legs. Anyone who knows a big old dog will know exactly what I mean. As he headed outside, he met Ocho bouncing off walls on his way in. They both knew the other was there, but Charly's arthritis meant that he could not move quickly enough to avoid his old adversary's stumbling approach, and Ocho could not see where to go. The result was an embrace that embarrassed them both.

So, we are facing new challenges as the animals get older, and I am sure there will be many more to come – challenges, that is, not animals. The top shelf of the pantry is devoted to the animals' medicines: Charly's for his arthritis, Tintin is prone to ear infections and Niña's bit of spaniel has given her old watery eyes that benefit from eye drops. In contrast, our bathroom cabinet has a packet of aspirin past its sell-by date and a tatty box of plasters, so at least the dogs keep us fit.

Regular visitors to this area often remark that they see far fewer strays these days, at which point Stephen usually mutters something like 'that's because they all live with us'. The diaries that I started keeping almost three years ago record the fact that in 2007, our first year of fostering, we took in one hundred and twenty-three kittens and puppies; 2008 brought us a further one hundred and nineteen. Hopefully, the fact that last year the number had dropped to eighty-six is a sign that the neutering programme is beginning to work. Time will tell. But all of that, as they say, is another story.

Acknowledgements

I will keep my thanks brief and skip the bit about my parents for having me and my family for their unwavering support. Family have little choice.

However, friends have the option. Thank you Chester Wolford, an American professor of English literature, for the generosity of his advice and his friendship. Anne Wright and Gil Woolley for never letting me take myself seriously and for always having chilled Chardonnay in their fridges.

Thanks, too: Tim Carroll, an established author prepared to give the new kid an introduction to Mainstream Publishing; Bill Campbell for taking the gamble; Karyn Millar, who gave this mongrel of a book a touch of pedigree; and Emily Bland, who designed a cover that can still bring a tear to my eye.

Finally, and in a way, most importantly of all, thank you Charly. Had my first dog turned out to be the hound from hell, the rest would never have followed.

If you would like to look at our holiday homes, please visit our website: http://www.whitewashedwalls.com

Library Link Issues (For Staff Use Only)

1	2	3	4	5	6	7	8	9
					6724			

17467